THE WORK SMARTER GUIDE TO PITCHING

David Kean &
Tanya Khandurova

Series Editor David Kean

ROBINSON

First published in Great Britain in 2025 by
Robinson

10 9 8 7 6 5 4 3 2 1

Copyright © David Kean and Tanya Khandurova, 2025

The moral rights of the authors have been asserted.

All rights reserved.

No part of this publication may be reproduced, stored in a retrieval system, or transmitted, in any form, or by any means, without the prior permission in writing of the publisher, nor be otherwise circulated in any form of binding or cover other than that in which it is published and without a similar condition including this condition being imposed on the subsequent purchaser.

A CIP catalogue record for this book is available from the British Library.

ISBN: 978-1-4087-8318-4

Typeset in Sentinel and Scala Sans by Ian Hughes

Printed and bound in Great Britain by Clays Ltd, Elcograf S.p.A.

Papers used by Robinson are from well-managed forests and other responsible sources.

Robinson
An imprint of
Little, Brown Book Group
Carmelite House
50 Victoria Embankment
London EC4Y 0DZ

The authorised representative in the EEA is
Hachette Ireland
8 Castlecourt Centre, Dublin 15, D15 YF6A, Ireland
(email: info@hbgi.ie)

An Hachette UK Company

www.hachette.co.uk
www.littlebrown.co.uk

Tanya:
*To David.
His perfect pitch makes me say 'yes'
again and again.*

David:
*To Miles Young.
Simply the best client I ever had.*

Contents

FOREWORD: PITCHING IS EASY, ISN'T IT? — ix

PART I: PRE-PITCH — 1
1. What is a pitch? — 3
2. Planning the basics — 5

Checklist — 13

PART II: PEOPLE ARE PARAMOUNT — 15
3. First meeting with a prospect — 19
4. Personality styles and communication preferences — 23
5. Getting on the same wavelength — 31
6. It's not just about them – it's about us too — 38

Checklist — 41

PART III: PITCHING LIKE A PRO — 47
7. Process — 49
8. Promise — 56
9. Problem — 64
10. Product — 74
11. Profit — 79

Checklist — 86

PART IV: PRESENTING YOUR PITCH	89
12 It's showtime!	91
13 Control everything you can	97
14 Presenting a written pitch	112
15 Postscript	114
Checklist	116
PART V: POST-PITCH	117
16 You have just left the room	119
17 Lose or win – get feedback	124
18 When you win	126
Checklist	129
Acknowledgements	131
Index	132

FOREWORD

Pitching is easy, isn't it?

'Sierra Echo niner-seven-six Charlie Foxtrot, you are cleared to land at Helsingborg.' We could hear the chatter between our pilot and the control tower over the headsets we'd been given on our twenty-minute chopper ride across the Sound between Denmark and Sweden. Three days before we'd been invited to come and meet the owners of the nicotine-replacement therapy chewing gum Nicorette. The meeting was scheduled for one hour, just after lunch and there were three of us from our company in London – Michael, the irascible head of our international division; a strategist called Mark; and David, the co-author of this book. The management team greeted us hospitably and we took them through our fifteen-minute presentation – all verbal, no slides – which outlined our observations and thoughts on how to launch the gum in the UK. We could see that they were intrigued by the insights we'd generated from research groups over the intervening seventy-two hours and that they had fallen in love with our strategist (he was brilliant that day). After our presentation, they put their heads together and quietly consulted each other for a minute. Then they looked up at us across the table and said: 'We like what you have told us. We would like to proceed with you. Can we talk terms?' David and Mark discreetly left the room – this was a commercial conversation and only one person on our team could make that call: Michael.

Ten minutes later, Michael emerged, looking stunned. Silently, we walked to the helipad and got in. As the rotors began spinning and we slid the headsets over our ears, Michael mouthed, 'A quarter of a million pounds!' As we rose into the air, and as Helsingborg disappeared into the distance, the three of us dissolved into laughter and smiles. 'This pitching lark's easy, isn't it?' Mark beamed. 'I don't know why you make all that fuss over it, David.'

If you're lucky, you'll get one experience like this in a lifetime of pitching. When it happens, it's unforgettable. The rest of the time, you make your own luck. Here's how.

PART I
PRE-PITCH

'Victory loves preparation'
SENECA

CHAPTER 1
What is a pitch?

We pitch all the time – our ideas, vision, skills, products and services. We pitch for money, support, time, partnership and attention. We pitch to venture capitalists, private equity, clients, would-be-clients, partners and colleagues. Even to friends and family. Pitching is a vital business and life skill and full of drama – as the TV programmes *The Apprentice* and *Dragons' Den* can testify.

This book is not about being the Pied Piper of Hamelin where you put people under a spell and they all follow you as though in a trance. A pitch brings people around to your way of seeing the world, gets people to support that view and accompany you on the journey to where you are trying to get to. But it also needs to take into consideration what *they* want, where they are going.

We believe in cooperation. In our human desire to progress and find a way to do something *together* – to be part of something, to have a sense of belonging. The other party has to feel free that it is *their* decision. You have to know who you're talking to, what they need, what you need, and where you overlap. Because persuasion isn't about getting what you want at any cost. It's about getting what you want in a way that leaves both of you better off.

Here's an example of what we mean. When the film director Richard Attenborough didn't like the way an actor was delivering a scene and wanted them to play it differently, he would talk them through how he envisioned the scene and ask them to try it that way. But after he expressed his preference, he always said, 'Of course, it's entirely up to you!' He gave them a choice. And by giving them a choice he allowed them to feel agency in the decision – enough agency not to feel coerced. And, every time, the actor tried it. Every time, it was better. Attenborough always got his own way. But the actors felt they'd made the decision.

The stakes are often very high: 'Will you marry me?' 'Will you be my partner?' 'Will you give me the job?' 'Will you join my team?' 'Will you give me your business?' 'Will you invest in my enterprise?' Pitching and persuasion are what make our worlds go round. So you need to be good at it when it matters.

This little playbook of persuasion will help you to pitch with structure and confidence. Whether you are chasing a big business deal, securing investment, winning votes or simply persuading your family to go on a holiday adventure, this book will help you win.

You will save time and money, and avoid frustration, by learning a smarter way to pitch. Each section tells you *what* to do and *how* to do it, with practical checklists to keep you on track. It will help you not only win but also 'live happily ever after'.

CHAPTER 2
Planning the basics

First, don't get the basics *wrong*. Any pitch will fail if you do. We have seen it time and time again.

If you stick to several basic principles and don't deviate from them, then you have a much greater chance of winning.

But everywhere we go, we see people pitching wrong; people professing they want to win and then doing everything they can to prevent that. They waste time, start late and get sidetracked. They do things last minute and fail to rehearse. Then they wonder why they lose. Without good methods and practical tools, pitching gets chaotic and victory becomes far too random.

Everyone wants to nail the big idea. They rush to the solution as it's the interesting bit. But very few think about the basics.

We win a pitch because we make an impression. When we lose, it is seldom because of a grand critical error. Even the best pitches die by banal blunders, by small, stupid mistakes. You'll never get everyone to love the same thing, but what turns people *off* is almost universal. Disappointment often follows a familiar script.

So, before you dive into the interesting stuff, take a moment to make sure you are not screwing up on the simple stuff. Don't give your client an easy reason to say no.

1. Show your enthusiasm from the very beginning – demonstrate it, don't just say it

You've been invited to pitch, asked for a proposal or just given a chance to talk – so act like it matters. Thank them right away. Show you're excited and that you know this is important, both to you and for them. Show that you're eager, because enthusiasm makes a good impression and sets the tone for real partnership.

For example, when we turn up to a first meeting with a new business prospect, we always open our notebook so the client can see our preparatory notes for the meeting. That way, they know that we have thought about this meeting, prepared questions to ask and specific information we think they might want to know. And we write down what they tell us – not just so we remember what they say, but to signal to them that what they are saying is valuable.

Clients love to talk. Let them talk and be visibly fascinated.

Here's another illustration of the need to exhibit enthusiasm rather than merely say it. We were pitching for the global business of UPS, the logistics giant. One of UPS's board members had a sit-down for thirty minutes with our CEO. We asked for a debrief of the conversation and heard that the UPS executive had said to our CEO, 'It's such a shame you cannot find time in your diary for a visit to WorldPort.'

WorldPort was the throbbing heart of UPS's parcel distribution network, more advanced than any competitor's logistics operation. It was the company's pride and joy.

Our CEO hadn't thought any more about the comment but we immediately instructed him to *find the time* and get to WorldPort as soon as possible. Why? Because, reading between the lines of what the board executive had said was a coded message: 'You've lost the pitch'.

She meant: 'If you don't go to see WorldPort, you won't understand our business and so won't be able to help us – however clever you are.'

Our CEO found the time and we won. Clients love their product. You should love it too, and *show* you love it. Let your actions show your enthusiasm, not just your words.

2. Meet the client

There is an old saying: familiarity breeds contempt. Not in pitching. In pitching it's the opposite: familiarity breeds *favourability*. Fit in as many meetings as possible. You are not pitching in a vacuum. Pitching involves personalities and for chemistry to occur between personalities, for them to get on the same wavelength, they need to spend time together. So get in front of the clients, see how they react, and find out their attitudes, strategies, beliefs, hopes, fears and prejudices. Even pre-sell your solution before the big presentation.

It seems obvious, yet again and again we see people plunging into the brief and brainstorming solutions instead of scheduling meetings with clients. If they won't meet with you, then you're probably wasting your time – they don't care about finding the best solution. Either your competitor has an inside track and is meeting them covertly or you are in a lottery where it's anyone's guess what the right answer is. Pull out. No one has the time and money to waste on a lottery.

We've seen companies walk away from pitches because the client wouldn't meet with them. More often than not, the client calls back and agrees to have the meeting. (Suddenly they agree to the pitch *on your terms*.) Remember: clients are people, too. Sometimes they can be difficult. It's okay to push back and ask them what's more important: the process or getting the best result.

3. Dobble- and triple-checke everything

See what we did there? If you didn't notice the typos in the sub-heading above (and not everyone will), you need to run your written output past someone else who *does* spot that sort of detail.

We've seen management summaries from CEOs to prospective clients which contain multiple spelling mistakes. Do you think the full submission gets read if the letter hasn't even been spell-checked? No. Please – it's not difficult. Nowadays, there are so many tools to help you make sure your text is at least grammatically correct.

Check people's names and brand names multiple times. This is basic good manners. No one questions showing up in a clean shirt and knowing how to behave at the dinner table. It is the same with spelling, names, titles, pronouns, dietary requirements etc. Getting these little things wrong breaks the relationship before you even start.

4. Appearance

It's understood that in most business environments, dress standards are usually informal. But that doesn't excuse a careless approach to how you present yourself. Aim to be appropriately presented. (As a rule of thumb, be the smartest person you'll meet today.) We've been in situations where we had to run to the nearest shop for a clean shirt or hunt down an iron to make sure the team looked presentable. Think through your outfit carefully if you're on camera. Far too many people don't consider their lighting, their background, what others on their team are wearing, their distance from the camera or their sound level. And many people forget they are on camera. So when they're not talking, they lapse into low-energy mode: their facial expression drops and they look tired, or they work off two screens and fail to make eye contact, or they eat during the meeting so the other participants can only see the top of their head as they tuck in.

You're putting on a show: you need to be at your best. You're 'on TV' so be self-aware.

You also need to clarify the client's rules and expectations about the pitch delivery early on. Sometimes clients mention the date of the presentation, but do not tell you the specifics or the format. How much time will you get? What room and with what technology? Will it be in real life or online or hybrid? Will technical support be available? Can you get into the room early? Know what you're aiming at and what to expect.

5. Arrive early

Not on time or just in time. It's a tiny detail, but it saves you in so many situations. It's always a good mindset for important meetings and pitches to plan for what could go wrong. Because the truth is, what can go wrong will go wrong. Trains get delayed. Airlines lose your baggage. Someone might spill coffee on you, and you will need to change at the last minute.

If nothing goes wrong, those extra ten minutes are still important. They allow you to settle in, get a feel for the space and get into a calm state of mind. Even in your own office, things might be slightly different on a big day – new people, different setup. You will have time to notice and rearrange it for the better. Those extra few minutes will always give you an advantage.

Live by the adage: *five minutes early is ten minutes late*.

6. Bring in an outsider

Outsiders prevent groupthink and speak truth to power. We always recommend the involvement of an outsider. It doesn't have to be an expensive consultant who specialises in pitching. Often, it's enough to ask colleagues from another department, a friendly client, a good acquaintance or even a family member to cast fresh eyes over the pitch.

We're all creatures of habit. Just as we get dressed the same way in the morning, take the same route to work and grab coffee from the same café, we follow many habits at work too. We get so used to our routines that we often become blind to other ways of doing things. A fresh set of eyes from someone who isn't stuck in your routine can bring very useful improvements:

- at the outset when they can give a fresh perspective on the task
- as an expert to share relevant experience and speed things up
- as a proofreader or ghostwriter for important documentation
- to ask hard – or simple – questions the team might not think of
- to act as devil's advocate and challenge thinking
- to rehearse the presentation, sharpen what's being said and tell you when you're using terminology that others won't understand

We advised one of the largest accounting firms on their pitch for a special government commission. Being accountants, their pitch was full of technical jargon, complicated financial formulae and multiple three-letter acronyms. We pointed out that the panel adjudicating the pitch was made up of some accountants, but mainly of trade union representatives, a life peer with no track record in business and an HR specialist – people who wouldn't understand 90 per cent of what was being presented. This meant our client would fail to connect with them and lose their votes. We rewrote the pitch in plain language and focused on the things that would be important to these people.

Another thing that you may discuss with an outsider is the bigger picture of what's happening in the organisation or the industry. We are sure you know a lot about it yourself but it's always good to have a different perspective. For instance, how the time of the year, industry events or political situation may affect your client's state of mind. Sometimes pitching in December feels entirely different from pitching in January or in August.

7. Emotions

Your emotions are a huge asset – one of the most crucial business resources there is. And even though business books talk about them all the time, we still tend to put 'emotions' somewhere under the title of wellbeing. We tick that box and feel good, thinking, 'We care about the mental and emotional health of our people.' Yet, it's your emotions that truly convince others. It's the level of your own belief that inspires people. People buy conviction.

Emotions drive you and your team towards victory. Ask any Olympic champion how important a winning mindset is to actually winning. Talk to actors, musicians or anyone who steps on stage. Do they just show up at the right place and time, or do they prepare themselves emotionally before they go out there?

Emotions may also lead to making mistakes. When people feel

distracted, scared to speak out, defensive or down, this shows up in their behaviour and affects their decision making.

So check in with your own and your team's emotions regularly.

8. Be organised

The big thing is to start *now*. Far too many people sit on the pitch assignment and let hours, days and weeks go by before they give it the attention it needs. Things start shifting or don't go as planned, other priorities assert themselves and we end up working on the presentation the night before the final pitch meeting. Sound familiar?

Plan your pitch preparation right from the start and all the way to the end – and even beyond the end, to post-presentation follow-up. Even if it's just you involved (it's even easier then), block out dates and times in your calendar for each stage of preparation – for internal team meetings as well as interactions with the clients. You have very limited time. You must use every minute to your advantage. Yes, you've got urgent emails from other clients; colleagues are demanding your attention; you are needed in ten places at once. You cannot let these things get in the way. A pitch is a very unforgiving mistress.

Organise diaries. Send out meeting invitations, decide in advance which ones will be online and which in person, and where they'll take place. Set aside time for planning, gathering materials, developing and prepping, discussions, and at least three practice runs. If it's a written tender, swap rehearsals for final read-throughs. You can always cancel if you do not need one meeting or another, but get it in everyone's schedule first.

9. Discipline

Be honest with yourself. Can you plan every step and also follow through without delay? Can you stick to deadlines and show up on time for meetings? If you know this isn't your strong suit, find someone who's better at it to help keep you on track.

It's like agreeing to go for a morning run with a friend. You know that when it's freezing and raining outside, you'll hit the snooze button on your alarm, roll over and go back to sleep. But then, five minutes later, your phone rings: 'Where are you? I'm standing outside your door getting soaked!' You get up immediately. (Of course, you need to pick the right friend for that job.)

Good discipline, being systematic and being methodical will make pitching so much more enjoyable and effective. When your system kicks in and the pitch process runs on rails, everything is easier. And the more you pitch, the easier it gets.

CHECKLIST

- [ ] Enthusiastic 'thank you' email, letter, phone call.
- [ ] Run spelling, grammar and punctuation checks.
- [ ] Make sure you have spare clothes, stationery, computer cables etc.
- [ ] Assume that whatever can go wrong will go wrong.
- [ ] Block in your meetings (particularly those with clients) to arrive fifteen minutes early. Allow for bad traffic, train delays and other unforeseen circumstances.
- [ ] Bring in an outsider to notice your bad habits, sense check, ask questions, challenge.
- [ ] Assess your emotional resources.
- [ ] Monitor your level of 'winning' positive emotions.
- [ ] Plan activities to boost your positive emotions and energy levels and those of your team – especially just prior to meeting the client.
- [ ] Schedule all of your meetings and preparation time.
- [ ] Appoint a person to help you with discipline. Some people are naturally very organised – choose them.

PART II
PEOPLE ARE PARAMOUNT

'When dealing with people, remember you are not dealing with creatures of logic, but creatures of emotion'
DALE CARNEGIE

Who are you pitching to? It sounds simple, but when we ask this, the answers we hear are often: 'the public sector', 'small banks', 'venture capitalists', 'medium-sized businesses', 'private equity' or 'organisations with EBITDA of X'. Especially in the business-to-business (B2B) universe, clients are described as faceless entities.

But abstract, conceptual entities (even if legally recognised), don't make decisions. *People* make decisions. B2B is really P2P – **people to people**. Every pitch is about the people you're pitching to.

Why is it a problem to think of clients just as businesses?

Companies may outlive specific individuals, but pitches, sales and persuasion aren't about logos, legal entities or contracts – they're about humans. The phrase 'It's not personal, it's strictly business' – a famous line in *The Godfather* – is echoed across boardrooms all over the world. It couldn't be more ironic: business is *incredibly* personal. When you get a new job, you feel elated and on top of the world – you celebrate with friends and family. When you're made redundant, it affects your sense of self-worth just as much as your bank balance. You're down in the doldrums. TV programmes dramatise the human intrigue in series about business empires such as *Succession*, and the drama in *Dragons' Den* comes from the relationships between the dragons and the entrepreneurs pitching their products. Business is as personal as it gets.

In the end, real people – not AI algorithms – will decide whether to work with you. They'll either back you and your ideas or reject them. And people make business decisions based on relationships, trust and emotion, even when they think they're being purely rational. It's why, quite often in the pitch process, there'll be a 'chemistry' meeting in the initial stages, to see if you can get on with the client and them with you. (Chemistry meetings are also designed to help clients check if the people in your team get on with each other, too.)

Victory will go to the side that understands the client best

Understanding your audience is the art of pitching. To succeed, you need to understand your clients deeply – not just their company roles but their personalities, priorities and pressures. Ask yourself:

- What are their agendas?
- What are their hopes, fears and beliefs?
- How do they think and make decisions?
- What internal politics are at play?

Clients want to work with people they *like*, who *understand* them, and who *share* their ambitions. Like you, they have biases, assumptions and preferences. They appreciate effort and love being truly heard. In short, clients are human beings.

CHAPTER 3
First meeting with a prospect

We had been scheduled to have a pitch 'chemistry' meeting to see how well we got on with the client team. The meeting was at our office in New York. The visiting company wanted a partner who could help them expand overseas from their US base and acknowledged that their mindset was very US-centric. We asked our team what single impression they wanted to create in the minds of the visitors. 'The fact that we are from and understand different cultures around the world and can therefore guide this client as they expand around the globe,' they said.

When the visitors arrived at 4 p.m. – we were in the graveyard slot, when they had already visited three of our competitors that day – they were escorted up to the meeting room and told that on entering the room they would meet nine people who would be their team. But instead of doing the usual 'wedding line' of introductions, where everyone says their name and job title, each person would be waiting to meet them in a different part of the room. They were told that among the nine people were a cinnamon farmer, a hot air balloonist, someone who had climbed Mount Everest, a world-class pastry chef, a journalist, someone who'd been a police hostage negotiator ... you get the picture. In other words, people with day jobs at this company but whose passions spoke of their love of other cultures and ways of living beyond their job function. Personalities. So when the visitors entered the room, everyone met as interesting individuals – the perfect icebreaker to get the relationship kickstarted memorably.

All around the room, food from countries throughout Asia,

Europe, Africa and South America was laid out, all of which was traditionally eaten at teatime – 4 p.m. This was never referenced or pointed out. It was just there for the visitors to enjoy. The visitors did notice the tea (and the fact that it hadn't been mentioned, just done) and fed back that this was the best chemistry meeting they'd had. They had taken away a very strong impression that this was a company finely attuned to the ways of the world, full of interesting, talented people who 'got' each other and understood the clients' 'detail matters' culture, too.

Why can't we pitch the same way to everyone?

Because people are different. The more time you spend understanding your clients – what matters to them, their personalities, politics and preferences – the better you can tailor your approach. Like a good doctor, you need to ask questions, listen carefully and dig deeper.

Your pitch is not just about the final presentation – it starts from the moment you face the client for the first time. Think of each interaction as a stepping stone, incrementally pulling you ahead of the competition. It happens every time you have an interaction with the client – be it an email, conference call, chemistry meeting, Q&A session, breakfast, lunch, dinner or formal presentation to their board.

Your first impression sets the tone. You don't get a second chance to make a first impression. We have heard it a million times, but, surprisingly, the first client meeting is often the one we're least prepared for. We treat it as low stakes: draft a few questions, introduce ourselves and listen politely. The only preparation needed, it seems, is to talk about your business if asked. No need to prove anything yet, right?

Wrong.

Every interaction with the client is a mini-pitch. Each meeting offers an opportunity to stand out – or blend into the background.

Let us share a story. We worked for a creative agency. We landed a meeting with a promising potential client, a young and energetic marketing director. To impress, we brought in our top brass: the strategy director, creative director and client services director. Everything seemed perfect, or so we thought. The meeting was a pleasant, friendly conversation. We asked thoughtful questions, explained our methodologies and shared case studies.

At the end of the session, the client sighed and said, 'This is great, but I was expecting creative folks with mohawks and green hair ...'

We did not do the homework and missed the mark entirely. We didn't align with their expectations. Despite our expertise, the client didn't even send us the brief.

The lesson: if you don't prepare for the first meeting, you risk misunderstanding your client's needs – or worse, failing to resonate with them as people.

How to prepare for the first meeting with your client

It is much more than drafting questions. It's about understanding the client's expectations, assumptions and goals before you walk into the room. Try these three ways to ensure you're ready:

1. Ask the client directly

Sometimes the simplest approach is the best. Before the meeting, ask the client what they're hoping to achieve. What do they expect from you? Are there specific topics they'd like to cover?

This gives you clarity and also shows the client that you're proactive and invested.

2. Find an insider (your 'mole')

Leverage your network. Is there someone on your team or a mutual connection who already knows the client? They can provide valuable insights into the client's personality, preferences and expectations. We pitched for an assignment for the National Health Service in the UK. There are very rigid protocols about public-sector pitching. We knew a surgeon who knew a top civil servant in the Department of Health and Social Care, so we arranged a lunch with both of them. The civil servant helped us understand the personality of the commissioning client and that knowledge informed how we behaved with this person. It worked. Every other company pitching rubbed him up the wrong way. We got on like a house on fire.

Even in the most rigid process, you can always find a friend.

3. Build a diverse team

Casting is key. Forget rigid hierarchies. Instead of defaulting to senior leaders, or whoever happens to be available, assemble a team that includes diverse perspectives and personality styles. Include creative thinkers, technical experts and people with different communication styles. This way you'll have the right voices in the room and a much better shot at making a real connection.

The first meeting sets the foundation for your pitch, but it's only the beginning. Treat every interaction as a chance to deepen your connection. Whether it's a casual email, a conference call or a formal presentation, each moment is an opportunity to increase your advantage and get ahead of the competition.

CHAPTER 4

Personality styles and communication preferences

Your first meeting is the gateway to understanding your client. As you engage, pay attention to how they communicate, make decisions and interact with others. These observations will help you to identify their personality profile – the key to crafting a pitch that resonates.

Have you ever watched people in a coffee shop early in the morning?

At 8 a.m., on the dot, Anna strides in, looking like she's already conquered half her to-do list. Head down, thumbs flying over her phone, she barely glances at the barista. 'Large Americano, no sugar.' Waiting in line, she's all business, checking emails, eyes glued to the screen. Coffee in hand, she's out of the door before the first sip. Anna values efficiency, direction and speed.

Then there's Pardeep, walking in with a smile just as the espresso machine lets out a long, weary sigh. The café, still shaking off the last traces of morning drowsiness, stirs a little at her arrival. She moves with the ease of someone who belongs – not in a loud or commanding way, but in the quiet, natural rhythm of familiarity. 'Hey! Morning!' she calls, her voice warm, effortless. The barista, Luca, looks up, already halfway into a smile. 'How's your morning going?' Pardeep asks, and unlike most, she isn't just filling the space between ordering and paying. She listens, nodding, tucking away whatever little detail he offers. She collects her latte as if it were a letter from an old friend, settles by the window, and waves at another regular. To Pardeep, coffee is merely a vessel – what she truly savours is the company.

A bit later, Sam barges in, brimming with enthusiasm, as if her very arrival were some lively performance. She's on the phone and cannot stop speaking for a moment. The café is filled with her voice: vibrant and engaging, it cannot bear to leave any air unoccupied. 'Oh, hang on – I need my caffeine fix!' she declares with a nod to the barista who, knowing well the measure of her need, begins preparing the usual – a double mocha with (naturally) the requisite extra whip. Ah, but Sam is not done. With a beaming smile, she continues, laughing, gesturing grandly, and pulling in an unsuspecting nearby customer. 'You won't believe what happened last night ...' she stage whispers to the barista, as though the entire world were a stage and everyone in it an audience for her unfolding drama. For Sam, it's all about energy, shared and woven into the fabric of connection.

Finally, Alex enters with quiet deliberation and an air of purposeful detachment, as though she came to this establishment not merely to partake of its offerings but to observe the mechanisms that govern its small, contained world. She glances at the menu with a perfunctory air, confirming what she already knew, before requesting: a medium cappuccino with an extra shot. Her eyes linger on the nutritional chart, her gaze steady, yet distant – she is engaged in a mental calculation, weighing the unseen consequences of each choice. Upon receiving her coffee, she does not immediately indulge, but first tests its temperature – a gesture that suggests a mind attuned to the subtleties of life's daily rituals. Only then, with a careful, measured gesture, does she choose a seat. She is not, it seems, distracted by the trivialities of the world around her but rather engrossed in the fine-tuned precision of technology's unfolding trends – ever searching for what she needs to do to get things right. Anna, Pardeep, Sam and Alex represent different *behavioural styles*, or *personality types* as they are sometimes called.

Throughout history, countless personality typologies have been developed – from Hippocrates' classic sanguine, choleric, melancholic and phlegmatic types to more modern frameworks like Myers-Briggs,

DISC and OCEAN. For our purposes, we'll use a simple and practical system of four profiles.

Why does personality profiling matter so much? People process information, make decisions, and respond to ideas differently based on their deep-seated preferences. Adjusting to their style can be the difference between a lukewarm reception and an enthusiastic buy-in.

Does this mean we don't need to treat everyone as unique and that people can be boxed into a particular category? Not at all. Each person is a unique blend of many traits. However, most of us lean towards a dominant type in our communication and behaviour. While we're all trained to manage time and details, make decisions, lead and collaborate, the way we naturally approach these tasks can vary as much as our morning coffee orders.

Take holidays, for instance. Some are spreadsheet people, for whom every moment is meticulously planned. Others thrive on pure spontaneity, deciding on a whim to visit a place they saw in a movie.

Or consider birthday parties. For some, a surprise bash with costumes is a dream come true. For others, surprises are a nightmare – they need a clear plan, not unexpected chaos.

We're adaptable and can play different roles when needed, but each of us has a default mode – the way we're wired. There's no one-size-fits-all. In a company with strict rules for timed meeting agendas, some will think, 'Perfect, that's how it should be.' Others? They'll follow the rule, but they'll feel constrained.

Similarly, while some thrive on long and deep committee discussions, others prefer swift, decisive action.

Personality profiling exercises are often used for self-reflection. But their real value lies in something bigger – not just understanding yourself, but *learning to adapt your approach to better connect with others*. This is why, when pitching, it's crucial to know your audience. Who's across the table? What's their style? How do you connect with them quickly and speak their language? How do you get on their wavelength?

Once you grasp what drives people, you'll have those 'Aha!' moments where real connections happen.

Exercise: how to spot personality types

No, you can't hand out questionnaires to everyone you meet. But you don't need to. Clues are everywhere. Start with people you already know. Then try it with public figures, the ones you watch on TV or read about. Soon, picking up on behavioural styles will become second nature.

Let's think about people you know who:

1. Love a plan, love a schedule, love a spreadsheet

They need to know not just what we're doing, but also how we're doing it, when, and with what resources. They read the label – front and back – of everything they buy, including the ingredients, the source and the fine print. They check reviews and read the manual (yes, the whole thing). Perfectionists at heart, they hate making mistakes. If you ask them a question, even a simple one, expect a pause. For them, no question has a simple answer because everything should be weighed, balanced, questioned and researched before responding.

'Would you like a cup of tea?'

'Er ... Yes, I suppose, as I have been driving for a long time and it is not time for dinner yet, I could do with a small cup of tea with a dash of milk, no sugar.'

They like well-structured, well-prepared meetings with detailed agendas. Their birthday parties will have no surprises and tend to follow a similar script year after year. They thrive on predictability and routine. If you give them a painting as a gift, be prepared for detailed questions about the artist, the year it was painted, why and how ... can't they just enjoy it?! But for them, that *is* the enjoyment – having plenty of information to mull over.

How do they make decisions?

They research, study, make a plan with 'stepping stones' and handle everything themselves or, at the very least, check and proofread everything. That's classic **Analytical** behaviour.

Now think about family members, friends or colleagues who exhibit these behaviours and who you would describe as precise, careful, logical, thorough, attentive to detail on a good day – and as nit-picky, pedantic, boring or detail-obsessed on a bad day.

_____

_____

_____

_____

2. Driven by project objectives and outcomes, but move very fast

The manuals and instruction books stay in their cellophane, unopened. They quickly look at a new device, press a few buttons and figure out how it works. The rest is detail and doesn't matter to the **Driver**. They read only the headlines. They want something – they go get it. For Drivers, it's about achieving results. Their own opinion matters most to them. Do not argue with them – they will not stop until they win, even if they regret it later. When they talk to you, it may feel like they're talking *at* you. They hate time-consuming extensive research or committee votes.

'Cup of tea?'

'Yes. Let's get down to business.'

They prefer to make their own decisions and take full responsibility.

Everything has a purpose. A party? Sure, but only if it serves a specific goal – whether it's showcasing their new house, networking with neighbours or advancing professional relationships. For Drivers, even social gatherings must be meaningful. They mix friends, colleagues and family only if there's a clear purpose, and rarely just for casual fun.

How do they make decisions?

They announce their decision, set objectives and deadlines, and ask you to report on progress. They're not too concerned with how you get it done – as long as you get it done.

Now think about family members, friends or colleagues who exhibit these behaviours and who you would describe as goal-oriented, decisive, direct, determined and efficient on a good day – and as domineering, demanding, insensitive, bossy or dictatorial on a bad day.

_____

_____

_____

_____

3. Want to make everyone happy

We all know people who avoid conflict at all costs. Because of this, they're often bad at difficult conversations – such as delivering unpleasant news or giving negative feedback. They try to avoid such conversations as much as possible. At the same time, if there's conflict between others, they will do their best to bring people together. It seems almost impossible to annoy them or make them angry. But beware – they may not show displeasure directly (to avoid conflict), but that doesn't mean they aren't hurt, angry or won't eventually show it, possibly through passive-aggressive behaviour or non-compliance.

Like Analytical types, these individuals are good listeners. However, their listening is focused on people (rather than tasks). They do this with the genuine intention of creating a nice and comfortable environment rather than analysing new information for the best solution. They fit into nearly any group and don't feel the need to be the centre of attention or the leader in any team. They like sharing and doing things together. They are called **Amiables** – everyone's friend.

Their parties are relaxed and informal. They're happy to mix friends, family, colleagues and even new acquaintances – everyone is welcome, and the more, the merrier. In fact, there are no strangers in their world, only friends they haven't met yet.

How do they make decisions?

They don't – at least not alone. They have enough people around to do it for them. This is how they work – they gather a team and successfully delegate the decision-making.

Now think about family members, friends or colleagues who exhibit these behaviours and who you would describe as warm, accepting, patient, cooperative and friendly on a good day – and as indecisive, weak, time-wasting or lacking goals on a bad day.

_____

_____

_____

_____

4. Bring energy, excitement and enthusiasm

Like Amiables, they are people-oriented, but these individuals are happy to be the centre of attention. In fact, they often strive for it and are usually good at presenting and public speaking. They're natural networkers, full of interesting stories about everyone and everything. They love human interaction. Like Drivers, they love it when people listen to them, but others don't need to follow their lead or do as they say. They want people to admire them and applaud them.

Enthusiasm and involvement are critical for these **Expressives**. They are drawn to labels like 'newest', 'biggest' or 'best' – they never want to miss out on anything exciting or important.

How do they make decisions?

When it comes to decisions, they make them quickly and confidently – just don't ask them why or how they made their choice. They simply *feel* or *see* it. They have a clear vision of the big picture and know how things *should* be, but not how they should be structured or the specific steps to get there.

Now think about family members, friends or colleagues who exhibit these behaviours and who you would describe as creative, open, optimistic and energetic on a good day – and as overconfident, superficial, exaggerating or failing to follow through on a bad day.

We hope you've been able to identify most of your family, friends and colleagues through these descriptions. Remember, they don't have to tick all the boxes. In truth, everyone is a combination of all four types, but usually, one or two styles are most dominant. Try to determine which ones.

_____

_____

_____

_____

Important Note:

We use the terms Analytical, Driver, Amiable and Expressive for simplicity. These labels have nothing to do with people's human qualities, abilities or values. Everyone can analyse, drive, express themselves and be amiable. A Driver can be slower and be caring, particularly if their goal is to build consensus. An Expressive can focus on details, particularly on a creative and exciting project. We can all be caring, responsible, decisive, inspiring and much more. We just do it in different ways.

CHAPTER 5

Getting on the same wavelength

Now that you have analysed the personality styles of people you know well, what if you are meeting your prospective client for the first time? How can you identify their preferred style?

This is why you have your small-talk opening and first-few-minute rituals. For example: 'Are you sitting comfortably? Then let's begin.'

This classic fairy-tale opening is a typical Amiable approach. To start with, the Amiable tone – gentle, concerned and non-intrusive – works for everyone, even the Driver. Offer a genuine smile, a friendly 'How's it going?' and ask about their journey, the latest sports game or something that's big news that day. Small talk is your diagnostic tool; observe how they respond.

Analytical: cool, composed and detail-oriented

An Analytical arrives on time (or even early) and waits for you to initiate the conversation. If offered coffee, they'll likely specify their preference unprompted.

Every answer is measured and precise. They're thorough, deliberate and will embrace silence to give them space to think of the best response. If meeting at a restaurant, they'll study the menu carefully – perhaps even checking nutritional details. They expect clarity and specifics in return. Meetings with an Analytical are often prearranged with an agenda. They hate being unprepared and may bring slides, charts or spreadsheets to structure the discussion and validate conclusions. Expect phrases such as, 'according to ...' or 'based on these numbers ...' They prefer logical, structured language and value accuracy over speed.

What to offer: They value data and certainty. Offer them details, provide them with information and be their work partner.

Driver: direct, business-like and to-the-point

When asked, 'How are you?' the Driver's response is likely to be 'Fine, thanks,' and they will move on quickly. There's minimal small talk, if any. If offered coffee, the response is brief – 'yes' or 'no'. They don't want distractions.

In conversation, expect concise, direct answers. If they don't know something, they'll admit it without hesitation and look for a solution, not a discussion.

They're action-oriented and focus on results, often using phrases like 'let's get to the point' or 'the bottom line is ...' Drivers tend to dominate conversations, pushing for quick decisions. They dislike long discussions or unnecessary details.

What to offer: They're focused on results and efficiency. Be brief, be brilliant, be gone.

Amiable: relaxed, approachable and people-focused

Amiables thrive on small talk, especially when it's about personal topics. They'll ask about your family, your weekend plans or shared interests – and they genuinely care about your answers.

Their language is inclusive and caring: 'we', 'us', 'share'. They want to know how you feel, seek input and prioritise collaboration and harmony. Amiables value consensus and are patient, even with long discussions.

What to offer: They seek relationships and cooperation. Make sure everyone's voice is heard and maintain a friendly environment.

Expressive: lively, energetic and full of flair

Expect an enthusiastic greeting: 'How's everything going?' or 'What's new?' Expressives enjoy small talk, often jumping between topics and sharing stories. They may offer their opinion on the best local coffee spots.

They often provide engaging, detailed responses with colourful language. Phrases like 'imagine if ...' or 'wouldn't it be amazing if ...' are common. They focus on the big picture, are excited about possibilities and ideas, and thrive on interaction and connection.

What to offer: They bring energy and excitement to the conversation, encouraging brainstorming and lively discussions. They want connection and engagement.

What if you're meeting them online?

If you're meeting people virtually, start by doing some research. It's always helpful to know something about them before the first meeting. Look up their social media profiles and any articles, interviews or videos they've featured in – this will give you insights into their communication style and priorities.

Analytical

In online meetings, Analyticals prefer neutral or blurred backgrounds. They're often multitasking with multiple screens, looking at prepared documents, spreadsheets or slides. Eye contact is usually minimal, as they're focused on processing information. They may take notes or review data while speaking.

Their LinkedIn profiles often lack personalisation – expect formal role descriptions and detailed information about their achievements. They're thorough in documenting everything.

Driver

During an online meeting, Drivers appear focused, but their impatience is evident. They rarely engage in small talk and want to get straight to the point. If they don't care about something, they'll make it clear. Expect them to ask for the objective of the meeting right away, and to end it quickly once their goal is met. Online meetings with them are often transactional.

They also prefer to talk rather than listen.

Their LinkedIn profiles focus on achievements and results, not processes or details.

Amiable

Amiables bring a personal touch to online meetings. Their background may feature family photos, pets or personal items, making you feel like part of their world. A cat may come onto the screen. They're likely to ask about your background or your day. They'll nod, smile and be responsive throughout the conversation, valuing emotional connection and rapport.

Their social media profiles often emphasise teamwork, collaboration and community involvement. They take a more personal, friendly approach to networking.

Expressive

Expressives are animated and lively on video calls, often using their body and face to express themselves. They dislike blurred backgrounds and may dress in a way that reflects their personality. They enjoy the spotlight and want to engage with you.

They value enthusiasm and interaction, so they'll react with energy and positivity during the meeting.

On LinkedIn, they often share their stories with pictures and engaging content. They want to be seen and heard, thriving on the attention and connection they generate.

What happens when different people talk to each other?

Sometimes you immediately click with someone – you're in sync, understanding their point from the first words they utter and you finish each other's sentences. Then, there are those times when a productive conversation feels like hard work. You just do not seem to be on the same wavelength.

Imagine the following conversations. Do any of them feel familiar?

1. Expressive and Analytical

Expressive: I can just see this fridge in our kitchen. It'll be perfect!

Analytical (puzzled): What do you mean you 'just see'? Why this one?

Expressive: Trust me. It's the newest model. And I love the colour. It's exactly what we need.

Analytical (ready to fight): But have you read reviews? What new features are we paying for? Have you compared it with other models? Do we even need it now? Have you measured the space? Will it fit?

2. Expressive and Analytical (again)

Expressive: Would you like a cup of tea?

Analytical: A cup of tea? Well ...

Expressive (impatiently): Yes? No?

Analytical: On the one hand, I had tea recently, but on the other hand, it's been a long journey, so ...

Expressive has already gone to make tea ...

3. Driver and Expressive

Driver: I need you to finish that presentation. Deadline's tomorrow.

Expressive: Yeah, but I've got this awesome new idea to jazz it up.

Driver (shaking head): No jazz. Just stick to the plan.
Expressive (rolling eyes): But the jazz could make it pop!
Driver: 'Pop' doesn't land deals. Getting it done does.

4. Driver and Amiable

Amiable: Hey, how about we pause for a sec and just check in with everyone?
Driver (focused): We've wasted too much time. We need to move on.
Amiable: I share your frustration. But sometimes a quick chat with a whole team can speed things up.
Driver (reluctantly): Fine, but only five minutes. Let's not drag it out.

5. Driver and Analytical

Driver: We're launching the campaign next week. Done deal.
Analytical: Next week? I'm not sure we've covered everything in the plan.
Driver: We've covered enough. We can't sit on this for ever.
Analytical (frowning): But what about risks? Do we have a backup plan?
Driver: We'll handle it when it happens.

Just like when we travel to another country and learn a few useful phrases in the local language, learning how to speak someone else's 'personality language' is essential. It doesn't change who we are or manipulate anyone; it simply helps us be understood better.

We've all experienced moments where people talk too fast, too slowly or too much – asking too many questions, being overly indecisive or too excited. Our strengths can become weaknesses, especially in critical situations. Assertiveness turns into bossiness, thoughtfulness into pettiness, and patience into indecisiveness.

We constantly have to interpret not just the content of the message but the context and intent. It requires effort and skill to truly understand each other. If we do not, we misinterpret and miscommunicate.

Now that you know what communication style each type prefers, you should think of your clients and prepare your pitch in their language.

Presenting to a team

Very often we are pitching to a team. What do we do if we have several decision-makers and they all have different personality preferences? The rule is simple: provide everyone with what they prefer most.

Think about a well-designed print advertisement or a strong newspaper article. It has:

- A **clear headline** that communicates the key message for the **Driver**.
- A **picture** that illustrates the story for the **Expressive**.
- **Detailed text copy** that appeals to the **Analytical**.
- A **logo or the name of the writer** to build trust for the **Amiable**.

For the ideal presentation, it's important to sequence your approach.

- Start by addressing **Amiables** – make sure they feel comfortable and included. Even **Drivers** will tolerate a brief amount of small talk if it reassures them that everyone is on board.
- Then, clearly communicate the **objective** and **time limits** to the **Drivers**.
- Announce the **agenda** to the **Analyticals** and reassure them that you've gathered plenty of data, research and materials to back up your points (such as handouts or appendices).
- For the **Expressives**, tell a compelling **story** to capture their attention.

CHAPTER 6

It's not just about them – it's about us too

When pitching, it's not only about understanding your clients; it's also about understanding yourself and your team. Being aware of your own personality and how it interacts with those of your team members is crucial. Teams with diverse personality types tend to perform best, as they bring complementary strengths to the table.

The most challenging personality pairings in a team are **Analytical-Expressive** and **Amiable-Driver**, as their needs and communication styles differ significantly. However, teams that include all four personality types – **Analytical, Driver, Amiable and Expressive** – are the most effective, as they can navigate a wide range of client preferences and situations.

When preparing a pitch, aim to assemble a team with varied personality types. This diversity increases your ability to connect and build better relationships with clients, ensuring that everyone's communication style is effectively matched.

We are people too, so when we talk about people on the pitch we should not forget that like our clients we also bring our own assumptions and biases, our stereotypes, our experiences, cultural differences, languages, rituals and expectations. How we work together and whether we win or not very often depends on all of these factors rather than on job titles and the departments we work for.

How well do the gender, age and ethnic mix of your team match those of your client's team? How might national cultures influence our communication?

High-context cultures (Japan, UK, China, Arab countries) value *implicit* communication. The meaning of a message depends on context, relationships and non-verbal cues. Business conversations may start with indirect approaches. For example, in Japan, a meeting may begin with pleasantries and attention to formal protocols. Negotiations will not involve direct and open confrontation.

Low-context cultures (for example, the US, Germany, Scandinavia) prefer direct and *explicit* communication. Efficiency and clarity are top priorities, and there is little small talk or none at all. In some cultures the role of hierarchy is much more pronounced. In countries like China, Germany, India and South Korea, respect for rank and seniority shapes business conversations. Junior participants may be reluctant to voice opinions openly or may follow a specific protocol and wait for their turn to speak. In countries like Denmark, Sweden and the Netherlands, input will be sought from all team members regardless of rank.

Non-verbal communication is also different. In cultures like the US, eye contact signifies confidence and sincerity, while in Japan or South Korea, prolonged eye contact may be seen as disrespectful. Gestures considered friendly in one culture, like a thumbs-up, may carry negative connotations elsewhere, such as in parts of the Middle East.

Often, we engage in conversations with new prospective clients without taking into account these differences. Particularly if we operate on our home turf. We assume that if their company operates in London, Paris or New York, then they have fully assimilated and live by our norms. However, different languages and different cultural aspects are so deeply ingrained in us that if we want to communicate better we have to try and understand each other better.

What are our clients like when they come home? Do they eat with a knife and fork or change to chopsticks? Do they serve separate individual dishes or share plates and boards? What is the role of individuals and the community in their culture? What about gender roles? What are their attitudes towards older people, important people, children?

Different cultures can meet very successfully and produce wonderful results together if they recognise and respect their differences. When engaging in business conversations across cultures you should **research the cultural norms** of your counterparts beforehand, **be patient and observant**, especially in high-context or relationship-oriented cultures and **adapt your communication style** to match the cultural expectations.

As with national cultures, it is also important to understand *company cultures and languages*. Do they work in departments and hierarchies? How much horizontal cross-team communication is expected and encouraged? Are they laid-back? Are they task- and product-oriented or people-driven? What kind of discipline do they exercise – no one likes it when people are late, but for some companies it is a real crime, whereas in others they are more relaxed. Some companies are more creative and informal about their meetings. In other companies they prepare agendas very carefully and control time up to every minute – if your meeting needs twenty-seven minutes you are not supposed to book time for thirty.

These days the diversity of office cultures is huge – from working in office cubicles to special co-working spaces, from working from home to remote-working from a beach; all of these things matter for your pitch because they determine what is in the head of the decision-makers.

CHECKLIST

Conversation essentials for each personality type

Analytical
They want to consider all possible options and find the right one.

- [ ] Have a detailed agenda. If you make a presentation, start by explaining its contents.
- [ ] Summarise at the end. Follow the rule: 'say what you are going to say, say it, say what you have just said'.
- [ ] Present charts, spreadsheets, data – bring them *stuff*.
- [ ] Explain the route from problem to solution with clear milestones.
- [ ] Use bullet points.
- [ ] Expect a lot of 'what if' questions and also prepare your answers to what, why, when, where, who and how.
- [ ] Show proof for everything.
- [ ] Do not push for early answers.
- [ ] Use structure, logic and detail.
- [ ] Test and pilot projects.
- [ ] Debate and discuss everything from different angles and points of view.

EXAMPLE: DATA, EVIDENCE AND LOGIC
'This approach saves 20 per cent annually, supported by a detailed case study from a similar company.'

Driver
They want to make decisions and move on.

- [ ] Instead of small talk about the weather, check and manage time.
- [ ] Get straight to the main point.

- [ ] If you make a presentation, make sure your headlines communicate your points. Don't use generic headlines; they should articulate a point f view or move the argument forward. For example, 'The market is doubling every two months' rather than 'The market overview'.
- [ ] All charts, data etc. should be put in an appendix at the end, or given as handouts.
- [ ] If you use slides, use as few words and numbers per slide as you can.
- [ ] Be logical but skip detail and explanations.
- [ ] Align on aims, objectives, deadlines.
- [ ] Present options and leave the decision to them.
- [ ] Communicate clear actions and next steps.
- [ ] Never promise anything you are not prepared to do.

EXAMPLE: RESULTS AND EFFICIENCY
'We can implement this immediately to reduce lead times by 30 per cent and secure market dominance.'

Amiable
They want to discuss everything and reach an agreement (find a consensus).
- [ ] Small talk is a must.
- [ ] Have breaks.
- [ ] Keep the atmosphere friendly, collaborative and pressure-free.
- [ ] If you make a presentation, present the team – include photos and biographies.
- [ ] Acknowledge contributions and ideas openly to make everyone feel valued.
- [ ] Discuss and involve.
- [ ] Show flexibility.
- [ ] Check regularly on everyone's thoughts and feelings.
- [ ] Be ready to go over the allocated time. Avoid rushing them – allow time to process and consult others if needed.
- [ ] Reinforce shared goals and mutual benefits throughout the conversation.

- [ ] Use inclusive language that emphasises impact on others, teamwork and togetherness.

EXAMPLE: RELATIONSHIP AND COLLABORATION
'This solution will simplify tasks for your team, boosting morale and allowing them to focus on their strengths.'

Expressive
They want to be engaged and dream big.

- [ ] Show enthusiasm and energy – match their level of excitement.
- [ ] Make light-hearted small talk; show interest in their stories and passions.
- [ ] Use vivid, emotional language to create an exciting narrative.
- [ ] Be visually creative: use colourful slides, bold visuals and eye-catching designs if presenting.
- [ ] Share the big picture first, focusing on vision, and don't suffocate them with detail.
- [ ] Ask them for their ideas and show how much you appreciate their opinion and input.
- [ ] Use stories, analogies or examples to make points relatable and memorable.
- [ ] Avoid overly rigid structures or dull data – inject fun and spontaneity. Keep the tone friendly, optimistic and forward-looking.
- [ ] Give them space to dream big.
- [ ] To ensure alignment, as details may get lost in the excitement, follow up.

EXAMPLE: VISION AND INSPIRATION
'Imagine your brand setting the pace in the industry – this solution will take you from strong to unstoppable, making your team the talk of the town.'

CHECKLIST

What you need to know about the client and about yourself

Finding out what makes the client tick means you'll pitch in the appropriate way.

So here's the checklist of what you have to find out:

- [ ] Who the decision-maker is and what they want.
- [ ] Gender, age, ethnic mix.
- [ ] What is the language and the communication style the client employs – personality profiles.
- [ ] The company culture – the accepted behaviours, likes and dislikes, politics.
- [ ] Positions in the company (formal and informal).
- [ ] What makes them tick.
- [ ] What keeps them up at night.
- [ ] Assumptions/beliefs/biases/prejudices.
- [ ] Views and thoughts on the issue and possible solutions.
- [ ] Networks of people they (we) know.
- [ ] Background – personal and professional biographies.
- [ ] Hobbies, interests and other personal information.

How to gather this information

- [ ] **Do your homework:** Search their online presence – company websites, social media and industry articles.
- [ ] **Meet in person:** Face-to-face meetings activate parts of the brain that virtual meetings cannot and you are thirty-four times more likely to get agreement to a request in person than

in an email.[1] Trust is harder to build online, requiring more prep-aration and effort.

- ☐ **Find your insider:** Do you know someone with insights into the client's world?
- ☐ **Network smartly:** Does anyone on your team have a prior connection to this company or individual?
- ☐ **Ask questions like a doctor:** Probe, listen and probe again.

Success in pitching comes down to understanding people – what drives them, what scares them and what they care about. The team that digs the deepest into the client's world will always have the upper hand.

---

[1] Vanessa Bohns, 'A Face-to-Face Request Is 34 Times More Successful Than an Email', *Harvard Business Review*, 11 April 2017, https://hbr.org/2017/04/a-face-to-face-request-is-34-times-more-successful-than-an-email.

PART III

PITCHING LIKE A PRO

'Amateurs sit and wait for inspiration,
the rest of us just get up and go to work'
STEPHEN KING

CHAPTER 7

Process

Your pitch is not the final presentation.

Let's say that again, lest there be any doubt: your pitch is *not* the final presentation.

There's a horrible myth about pitching. Namely, that it's all about wowing them in the presentation. TV programmes like *Dragon's Den* and *The Apprentice* perpetuate this myth. They fetishise the five minutes you have in the boardroom with Lord Sugar or the multi-millionaires holding all the cash. Not because that's the only important thing but because car-crash presentations (or *very* successful ones) make for compulsive TV viewing.

This is wrong.

The presentation should be the coronation, the confirmation. When the curtain goes up and the audience sits in anticipation of a brilliant experience, the show in front of the audience is merely the culmination of a long process. The play has to be commissioned, written, financed and directed. This alone is not an easy process (watch the Oscar-winning film *Shakespeare in Love* if you want to get a glimpse into what has to happen before a single word is uttered on stage in front of a live audience). There has to be casting to get the right people to play the roles. Theatre productions don't just cast the people who happen to be available, but so many companies do in their pitches. There will be rehearsals. Over and over again. Rewrites. And then there's the music. The special effects. In the case of the *ABBA Voyage* virtual concert in London, a specially commissioned arena had to be built.

Then there's the 'surround sound', the communication with the public and the critics. With the listings sites. With the ticket intermediaries. On social media. Word of mouth. Previews. Reviews – both from professional critics and from the viewing public on social media platforms. There needs to be constant mood music to generate excitement and anticipation and encourage more and more people to buy tickets.

It's the *process* that generates success. Not just inspiration. Or a muse. Or luck.

It's exactly the same with your pitch. You must do all the necessary things in the pitch process to tip the playing field your way. Every email, every phone call, every social media post, every online meeting, every face-to-face with the client. And, just as importantly, with the people they trust and who they rely on – advisors, researchers, their R&D department, their lawyers, intermediaries, the media etc.

Those you are pitching to will be listening for 'echoes' – consistency of experiences they and those they rely on have had with you. Companies such as P&G, the multinational consumer goods conglomerate, tell their suppliers they are always listening for 'echoes' across different geographies to ensure that the standards of delivery are high all the time and everywhere. Dissonant echoes spell trouble for the supplier, because they mean inconsistency of P&G's experience. And P&G, like any client or venture capitalist or private- equity investor or TV producer, is looking for consistency of performance. Not for occasional brilliance.

This is why when it comes to your pitch process you should not rely solely on good habits and the organisational skills of individual people. Have a 'Pitch Playbook' specifically developed for your company. Every team member should have a copy and know how to use it. Police it. Make sure it is enforced.

The Pitch Playbook is a step-by-step manual to the pitch process in your company. It clearly states 'how we pitch round here'. It should include:

- Key stages of preparation and the time that needs to be allocated to each of them.
- A list of templates, manuals, presentations and other resources that can be used for your pitching process, including questions to ask and case studies.
- Descriptions of the different personality types, what they value and what type of communication they respond to best.
- A style guide for how documents and charts should be written.
- Internal procedures and frequency of team meetings to ensure the pitch is a priority and time is never wasted.
- Thinking tools to help accelerate your team towards a solution (e.g. PECSTEL – see p.71, and Six Thinking Hats – see p.75) with examples of how they have been used.
- Checklists of 'to do's, for example:
    - read the client brief/mandate/instruction every day
    - get meetings in the clients' diaries every week
    - set up daily team meetings
    - decide how to set up a meeting room when in your offices.

Things to consider

The client's process matters too. So your pitch starts from the first second you face the client and finishes long after you leave the presentation room. Your pitch process matters a lot. And in most cases you are not the only party that influences it. Timings, deadlines, presentation formats, Q&As, venues, decision-making steps, selection criteria and many other conditions of the pitch are often determined by the client. Get to know their processes.

Are you presenting **online or in real life**? The world has changed and online is playing a big role in pitching. It is very important to be aware that online and offline interactions work differently. They have different protocols, and your pitch process must be structured accordingly. We have heard a member of a pitch team bemoan the fact that she hadn't had much of a say in the pitch strategy because she worked from home and her colleagues were all in the office. She thought this wasn't very inclusive. But this is the harsh reality. If you're not in the room, you don't get a say. Pitches are hard work and part of the process is spending a lot of time together working. If your workstyle choice is to stay at home, you will miss the moments of serendipity when insight or breakthrough ideas come from personal interaction.

And if you are meeting in real life, do not waste time together staring at screens and slides for hours – this can be done online. Gather around the table, look at each other, play and role-play, rehearse, look and listen, use the physical space to move, group and re-group. Organise the space differently to promote dialogue and new perspectives. We usually remove the table from the room, which gives people a different experience, promotes openness and allows people to shape and reshape into different working groups easily.

Beware rehearsing online if your final presentation is in real life. And, of course, the other way around. If the pitch is going to be presented online then most rehearsals and even most team meetings should be online.

If you are meeting online, everyone in your team must join at least five (better ten) minutes early to test the technology. The role of an IT person may be different in the process online than offline.

Is the company you are pitching to **international** or **local**? Is it a local or international pitch? Have you allowed for different cultures and languages?

People may be speaking with different accents (sometimes heavy ones), have different small-talk protocols, different attitudes to time-keeping, etc.

What about different time zones? Where are you in their time of day? It may be midday for you but 8 p.m. for them. If so, they will be tired so you'll need to be energetic and your presentation should be light on charts – especially detailed ones. Even if you are in the same time zone, you might be their ninth consecutive meeting! It has happened to us before. How did we recover the situation? We abandoned the charts and asked what this person would most like to focus on.

Always think about how you may need to adjust your pitching process to allow for all of these nuances, to accommodate different needs.

Client criteria to win

Everyone has criteria for what they are looking for in a partner. If you don't know the criteria of the people you are pitching to, you're aiming at a target wearing a blindfold. Client criteria are a variable; knowing them from the very start is vital because they may affect the process. Find out how their criteria are weighted and what they prioritise. You need to find out early.

How do you find out? Ask! If they won't tell you, don't pitch. Why would you take part in a competition where you don't know where to aim? It would be a waste of time and money.

Using AI tools

There are many brilliant AI tools for pitching. But as with any useful tool, you must handle them with care. It is still your eye as the editor that prevents your pitch from sounding and looking templated. You will need to refine and tailor the work, get the tone right, match it to your company's or your own style, and make it human. Remember, the point is to stand apart at *every* stage of interaction with the people you are pitching to, so anything that sounds similar to your competitors' AI-generated pitches pulls you back into the morass of sameness you must escape in order to win.

Rehearse, rehearse, rehearse

THIS HAS TO BE THE NON-NEGOTIABLE, FUNDAMENTAL PART OF YOUR PROCESS. THE REHEARSAL DATES AND TIMES SHOULD BE FIXED IN EVERYONE'S DIARIES FROM THE VERY START.

True pitch champions rehearse at least three times. Why three times?

The first rehearsal, let's be frank, isn't really a rehearsal. Everyone comes into the room. You lay out your scribbled charts or put a draft presentation up on the screen, and you plod through the content. What you are doing is checking the sense, not rehearsing. You get your presentation into some sort of shape and some kind of logical order. (Hopefully.)

Too many people and too many companies stop there. They hope that everyone kind of knows what they're going to say and that, with a bit of individual practice in the shower on the morning of the presentation, it'll all be fine.

It won't. It never is. And we're not aiming for 'fine'; we're aiming for 'shine'.

Having re-briefed and edited the charts, you gather the team for another run-through. By this time all the presenters are familiar with *their* bit of the overall presentation. Each presenter does their bit, takes comments and goes off to amend their section. They concentrate purely on their content. This is why after two rehearsals you are just a group of individual performers that have come together. A group of individual performers always lose to the people who act like a team.

This is why you need your third rehearsal. This is where you produce magic. The third rehearsal is designed to make your show one seamless flow of brilliance. In your third rehearsal you must focus on those 'soft' areas – on behaving like a team, on projecting your enthusiasm, on signalling that they will enjoy working with you.

We will look at these aspects of presentation in more depth in Part Four (p.89).

In summary

Pitching is a process. It's about getting the small things 'righter' than the other guy, so they add up to a picture in the prospect's mind of you as the best. If their day-to-day experience of you is consistently sharp, high quality, error-free, timely, more engaging and memorable, and pulls you increasingly ahead of your competition in their eyes, well, you're headed for marriage.

We can't think of a slogan that sums this approach up better than the line the UK retailer Tesco uses in their ads: *Every little helps.*

CHAPTER 8

Promise

A pitch is a promise. It's not just about the idea or solution you're presenting; it's about the future you're inviting people to step into with you.

Think about it: when you pitch something – whether it's a business idea, a new product, or even yourself in a job interview – you're not selling the final version. Odds are, the idea will change. It'll get interrogated, prodded, played with, shaped, reshaped and, hopefully, improved by the people who buy into it. Very few solutions and ideas that are presented at pitch remain untouched by anyone else's input and come into the world exactly as you presented them.

Sure, your credentials, case studies and track record help. Those are your 'reasons to believe'. But what the people on the other side of the table are truly buying is *your promise of what could be achieved together*.

Ever proposed marriage to someone? You weren't selling the idea of 'today'. You were promising a shared *future*. A pitch is the same. Whether it's a client, an investor, a potential employer or a partner, they want to know: *where are you taking me?* If you can show them a shining city on a hill – a future that's exciting, achievable and worth the effort – they'll lean in.

In his 'I have a dream' speech, Martin Luther King didn't get bogged down in the *how*. Instead, he painted a vivid, emotional picture of what the future *could* be – a future so compelling that millions of people, black, white and of every colour, wanted to be part of it. It was a promise. (And what a promise!)

Your pitch works the same way. If your audience believes in your promise and sees themselves in your vision, you've won.

So, next time you're pitching, don't just sell an idea. Sell the promise. Sell the future. And make others believe it's a future worth having.

Whether the people make biscuits or biotech, they all want to believe they are on a mission more important than the mere product they produce. They want to feel they are doing something important. We once pitched for Easy Jeans – a family-owned apparel business. They claimed their jeans were every bit as well made as the brand leader. They felt it was unfair that customers should pay a vast premium to own a pair of 501s. We picked up on their sense of injustice and in the conclusion to our pitch we ended with a quote from a well-known campaigner for ethical consumerism:

> *I am still looking for the modern-day equivalent of those eighteenth-century Quakers who ran successful businesses, made money because they offered honest products and treated their people decently, worked hard, spent honestly, saved honestly, gave honest value for money, put back more than they took out and told no lies. This business creed, sadly, seems long forgotten.*
>
> ANITA RODDICK, FOUNDER OF THE BODY SHOP

Our last sentence in the pitch was: 'Well, that creed is not dead in this room. It's sitting right here in front of us. And we believe in it, too. Let's take this creed back into the world together.'

You could see in their faces that they were proud we had noticed their values. We walked out with the business because we showed them a vision of our future together, united in a common purpose and with shared beliefs.

Think about what you can promise to the client that corresponds to something they desire or already feel about themselves. When we pitched to UPS, we worked out very quickly that they needed a partner to help them navigate the world beyond North America and who understood the business-to-business world overseas. So everything we did was designed to signal our cultural sensitivity within different geographies and to underline our smarts in business-to-business communication. The final decision came down to the client's belief in the promise we made – which was backed with evidence – that we were the best guide to lead them into their new, international future.

Knowing yourself, understanding your audience and creating a compelling promise is the key formula of your introduction. Introducing yourself and introducing your team is an extremely powerful moment.

The power of introductions

Introducing yourselves is your first shot at connection, standing out from the crowd and setting the tone for what comes next. And yet how often do we really get it right? It's not just a chance to say, 'Hi, I'm here.'

We're given opportunities to introduce ourselves constantly – in meetings, at events, during pitches. It's an everyday part of life. Most of us fumble it. We use the same tired formula: name, job title, how long we've been at the company. Name, rank, serial number.

It doesn't offend anyone. The problem is, this standard introduction goes in one ear and out the other. It doesn't spark curiosity or make anyone think, *I want to know more about this person*. It's not that those details don't matter at all – it's just that they don't *connect*.

When you introduce yourself, you're not just giving a résumé summary. You're answering bigger questions: *Who are you? What do you stand for? Why should we care?*

Next time, skip the bland opener and give them something memorable. Instead of, 'I'm MG, the data manager,' try: 'I'm MG, and I help companies tell stories that double their sales.' Or: 'I'm MG, and I turn data into insights that make decisions easy.' You've instantly piqued interest and shown what you bring to the table.

Remember what makes us human. People don't just connect to *what* you do – they connect with *why* you do it. Share an anecdote to reveal passion, or a value that drives you. For example, we heard an entrepreneur from Nepal introduce himself and his business pitch to a panel of venture capitalists on the London Business School's *Launchpad* programme by saying: 'A million people leave my country every year because they can't get low-skilled jobs. That's a lot of families that get broken up and fathers who have to live apart from their children. I have a scheme to help a thousand people stay in Nepal with their families, earn money and also reduce our carbon footprint, make transporting goods around the Himalayas more efficient and deliver a 30 per cent margin. My name is Venkat Agarwal – would you like to hear more?'

Your introduction should fit the context. In a business pitch, highlight the role you'll play in solving the problem you've identified. Replace 'Hi, I'm Lisa, and I've been with XYZ Tech for eight years as a systems analyst' with 'I'm Lisa, and I stop companies from becoming tomorrow's headline news about a data breach.' It's a much stronger start.

The same goes for team introductions. When you're pitching with a group, don't just line everyone up to recite their titles. Use the moment to highlight what each person brings to the promise you're making. Make it clear why this team is the one that can deliver. For example: 'I'm Sarah, and I'll be your point person for project management. I will make sure we hit every milestone on time and on budget.' You're immediately signalling that you're hands-on, reliable and focused on your client's success. Or: 'I'm Mark, and I'm here to help you optimise your supply chain and future-proof it for the growth you're aiming for in the next five years.' This way your role matches their aspirations; you're positioning yourself as a long-term, valuable partner.

Introducing your colleagues rather than introducing yourselves is another way to differentiate your team and to signal how well you know, respect and like each other. We worked with a mergers and acquisitions firm who differentiated themselves right from the off by doing this. Introducing each other allowed them to sing the praises of each colleague fully and avoid the embarrassment many feel at singing their own praises. It also signalled that they knew and liked each other. They described each other as pieces on a chess board:

> Gunther is our leader and on our chessboard, the king. He doesn't move too much but when he does it is really significant.
> Carsten is our knight. He moves laterally and can leap over obstacles.
> Elske is our bishop. She thinks diagonally and gets to places others cannot reach.

We have never forgotten the first time we heard them do this. We saw seven firms present their credentials that morning. God they were tedious. These guys weren't. We're still in touch.

If your team introduction relies on written bios and photos, the same principles apply: every detail should support the story you're telling. And here a lot of team intros stumble – the photos. Too often, teams default to stiff, corporate headshots pulled from the company website. This is about *connection*.

Remember, pitching is matchmaking. You're not just selling an idea; you're building trust and chemistry with your potential client. The images you use should help you do this. You'd lavish care and attention on how you looked, smelled and sounded on a first date, wouldn't you? Your physical image matters. Your photo image is no less important. Think of it as part of your first impression (because it is).

Avoid lifeless passport-style headshots. Choose photos that feel human, warm and relatable. Ultimately, your photos should do more than show what you look like – they should suggest who you are as a team and why you're the right fit for this specific partnership. It's a small detail, but in pitching, small details often make the biggest impact (remember the 4 p.m. tea laid out from different parts of the world).

The same goes for personal biographies and the way you write about your team. Many pitch documents have been cobbled together from different sources and written by different people – from different departments, in different geographies and with differing styles and competencies in language. The end result is often not pretty. You need an editor-in-chief who can knit this jumble together into a succinct, readable, coherent whole.

If team résumés are just pulled off a central database, they won't be tailored for the intended audience. They'll be full of irrelevant information and miss the opportunity to create a word picture of a personality who will add value, who is committed and who wants to work on this project.

Below is a dull and undifferentiated example:

> *Ambitious senior IT leader and enterprise architect with global experience of medium-sized enterprises through to multi-billion $ corporations. Business-focused and commercially aware, with a broad technology and solution background.*
>
> *Driving the digital transformation agenda, shaping and delivering strategies and programmes from ambiguous and uncertain requirements, engaging with stakeholders up to C-suite to deliver true business value. Able to look at the big picture, manage the hype cycle and build a consensus using a straightforward, collaborative and open approach from conception to realisation.*

Ghastly, isn't it? A multitude of polysyllabic jargon words strung together in an incomprehensible word-salad of nonsense. (Ask yourself: when did you stop reading?)

What's the point of writing anything if it's not going to be read? Do you know what the mission of a good writer is? To get the reader to want to read the next sentence.

That's it.

Try this for size instead.

> *I am not entirely normal. Parachute me into a team in any market and I will survive, thrive, lead and enjoy every moment of it. I have managed businesses and IT projects in the UK, Russia, India, the US, Romania, Hungary, Greece and Turkey. I've built technology teams, overseen company acquisitions and led projects for the most famous brand in the world and delivered training for the world's biggest retailer in Arkansas. I studied experimental psychology and data science at Cambridge. My grandfather was a gypsy.*

Who would you rather meet? (If it's the former, go away – you're not ready to win more pitches.) By the way, they're both the same person.

And in case you're thinking, *I could never write such a thing – I'm a professional working in a serious business with serious clients who have serious challenges*, ask yourself how many pitches you're winning right now. QED.

Usually, in your submission, you will have to write an introduction to the team's résumés. Use it to explain what unites them all and why they want to work on this project together so badly. Mostly, this opportunity is thrown away in a stream of platitudes. Here's an example:

INTRODUCTION TO THE TEAM
We are honoured to have been selected to pitch for

McDonald's. If we were to be fortunate enough to win this assignment, you would be our largest client and our biggest new business win in a decade. In putting this team together we have handpicked the very finest talent and brains from within our international organisation. This pack contains a biography of each member of the team we are recommending, showing their competencies and the specific skillsets they will bring to you. Ranked number three in the EMEA market, we have the depth of resource and logistical capability to transition the business very rapidly in a matter of weeks so we can be up and running from day one. We pride ourselves on our talent and this is, along with our industry-recognised proprietary tools, what we believe differentiates us from our competitors.

Yawn. They would say that, wouldn't they? Try this, instead:

For us, it's personal

McDonald's. For every person on this team this has been a career-defining moment. Only once in our working lives are we likely to get the opportunity to work for a brand we have all grown up with, has been part of our personal stories and which offers the largest canvas on which to do the finest work of our lives. For every one of us, this is personal.

And before you cry, 'Aha! But I can use AI for writing now!', bear this in mind: by all means, use it. But like all writing technology – a quill, a pen, a typewriter – this wonderful tool will not give you the result you want if you do not know what you are looking for. *You have to know what good human language looks and reads like first.* You do not merely want your words to be smooth and perfect and delivered quickly. You want them to help you *connect* with your audience. And that takes craft.

CHAPTER 9

Problem

'If I had an hour to solve a problem, I'd spend fifty-five minutes defining it and five minutes solving it'
ALBERT EINSTEIN

Solving the problem. Presumably you are good at this. It is your craft skill – law, accountancy, real estate, marketing, sales, consultancy, investment, finance, architecture, technology, communications, production, manufacturing, training. The interesting bit. The knotty problem that you pride yourself on being able to solve. This is where you will win the pitch. But also, if you are not very careful, lose the pitch. Before you even start working on your solution (your 'product') you have to study the problem very thoroughly.

If your pitch is based on the client's brief/instruction/mandate – what it's called will depend on your industry – start with that. Remember, there will be as many interpretations of the brief as there are eyes on it. Different people interpret the same information differently based on their perspectives, experiences and assumptions. Acknowledging and addressing potential interpretations helps you to consider different perspectives. It also ensures you do not miss any detail or small print.

If you don't have a clear formal brief from your prospective client or investor, you still have to understand the *need* they have. What are they *really* looking for? This is not as easy to answer as it seems. You can, of course, ask them directly (and you should). But you must also always remember that very often they will tell you what they *want* and will not necessarily articulate what they *need*. So you have to work it out.

1. Read the brief *carefully*. If the client provides supplementary materials (such as reports), review them thoroughly for insights and constraints. This is particularly important in highly regulated markets or industries such as financial services.

We once got the brief of a lifetime – straight from our dream client. This was the big one: a world-famous brand, the kind of company you name-drop at parties. Naturally, our team dived in head first. The brief was crystal clear. It was also accompanied by a three-hundred-page research report that could double as a doorstop.

The creative team, buzzing with ideas, skimmed the report's summary and off they went to conjure their masterpiece. It was going to be *brilliant*. Award-worthy. Champagne-popping stuff.

But then there was *that guy*. Mr Detail, the Analytical account manager. While the rest of us were sketching genius concepts, he was holed up reading the entire three-hundred-page report. Every. Single. Page.

Fast forward to the rehearsal of our presentation. The creative team unveiled a concept so dazzling, so perfect, that the room broke into applause. Except for Mr Detail.

He cleared his throat. 'Page 267,' he said.

The room went silent.

'What about it?' someone asked.

'Page 267 explains why this idea – if executed – would be a PR disaster for their brand.'

It turned out, buried in the dense research was a single insight that would've torpedoed our entire pitch. Our 'masterpiece' could've sunk us – and our dream client along with it.

Never underestimate the power of page 267.

Make sure that at least one person in the team **reads every**

single word, including the small print, worries over the client brief all the time, keeps coming back to it and ensures that every single item on the brief is answered.

2. Clarify: What is the client's pain point or challenge? Look beyond what is explicitly stated to understand the underlying issue. Do not forget that nearly every word is polysemantic, i.e. has several different meanings. Even in our day-to-day and face-to-face conversations we very often misunderstand each other. Our business world is full of abstract words such as 'culture', 'transformation', 'innovation' and so on. If you ask ten people in the room to explain to you what each one means you are likely to have ten different explanations. When you pitch, you need to know for sure what they mean.

We once got a brief from a client that explicitly said they wanted 'creativity' at the heart of their 'cultural transformation'. It was there in black and white: *creativity*. Clear as day.

We were thrilled. This was our bread and butter. We sketched out ideas for open spaces, brainstorming hubs and training programmes to 'unlock creative potential'. Everyone was buzzing, picturing a Google-like playground where innovation and creativity flowed freely.

During an early discussion with the client, we threw out a question almost as an afterthought: 'When you say *creativity*, what does that mean for your business?'

Their answer stopped us in our tracks: 'We're not looking for artsy thinking,' they said. 'For us, creativity means rigorous problem-solving – data-driven but unafraid to challenge assumptions and biases. It's not about beanbags; it's about measurable results. Creativity grounded in practicality.'

When they said 'creativity', they didn't mean a wild explosion of ideas. They wanted disciplined ingenuity – a precision-engineered process to solve tough challenges. The type of 'creative culture' we'd envisioned wasn't just off-target; it was in a completely different part of the universe.

Words such as 'creativity' are like ink-blots. Everyone sees something different. For some, creativity is Picasso. For others, it's a Rubik's cube. And the only way to avoid running in the wrong direction is to ask questions – lots of them.

Think about it like this: if a hundred people were asked to draw a pig, you'd end up with a hundred different pigs. Some would be side-on, others front-on (some arse-end-on – yes, we've seen those). Some with curly tails, some with no tail. The same thing happens with words like 'creativity', 'transformation' and 'collaboration'. Each person's interpretation is shaped by their experiences, biases and the context.

So, if you're working from a brief, never assume everyone sees the same pig. Start by rephrasing what you've read. Say, 'Here's what we think you mean – are we right?' Because nailing that shared understanding isn't just the start of the pitch – it *is* the pitch.

Rephrase the brief back to the client during early discussions to confirm mutual understanding. Agree the brief as a priority – it'll save grief, reworking and money further up the track.

3. Read between the lines: check the context of the brief by looking at the client's brand values, industry trends and regulatory constraints.

Every conversation has two layers: the message and the context. Understanding both is the secret sauce of effective communication. The message is the straightforward part – the words spoken or written. But the context? That's where the real story unfolds. It's the emotions, history, culture, tone and environment wrapped around the words which quietly shape their meaning.

Miss the context, and you're in trouble. In British culture, the phrase 'It's not bad' can be glowing praise. 'This needs fixing.' Is it a stern rebuke? A helpful suggestion? The tone, timing and setting decide that. Even the simple 'I'm fine' can swing from 'Leave me alone' to 'All is well', depending on non-verbal cues like facial expressions or posture.

If spoken language is tricky, written communication is an

obstacle course. Words lose the benefit of tone and body language. Saying 'no' in person might involve a dozen subtle ways to soften the blow – hesitations, gentle phrasing or a sympathetic smile. In writing? It's just 'No.' Full stop.

As George Bernard Shaw famously said, 'The single biggest problem in communication is the illusion that it has taken place.' That's the danger of ignoring context: you might think you've nailed it when, in fact, you've completely missed the mark. It's the unspoken – the shared understanding of context – that makes the difference between clarity and confusion.

In order to understand your client's brief, you really have to dig deeper into:

- Cultural context: company culture and national culture if necessary;
- Historical context: history of the question;
- Situational context: the present situation and client's current challenges.

Again, you have to talk to them. Do not forget that very often people cannot explicitly include everything in a written document. They have lots of different restrictions too. Imagine a company posting a job vacancy for a quiet, thoughtful person who will just deal with paperwork and maybe make a decent cup of tea for colleagues? No job ad will ever read like that. It'll be packed with buzzwords like 'thrive under pressure' and 'dynamic, fast-paced environments'. It is your task to decipher what they're *actually* asking for. Because if you show up to the interview talking about how you're 'eager to change the world', they'll probably nod politely while mentally crossing you off the list. Even if the ad says they're 'looking for a young, ambitious person', you need to match the 'ambition' with the context of the role.

4. Challenge the challenge: When a client hands you a challenge, what they're really giving you is *their take* on the problem. It's filtered through their assumptions, blind spots and whatever slice of the picture they're working with. If you just run with that, you're gambling. You might end up solving the wrong problem – or worse, only scratching the surface of the real issue.

The problem the client states may not be the real problem at all. The problem in the brief may be a symptom of a deeper, unarticulated issue.

Example: The brief says, 'We need a rebranding to attract younger audiences.' You dig a little, and what do you find? Their real issue isn't branding – it's that their products are stuck in the past and irrelevant to customers under the age of thirty. You've got to look beyond the obvious to uncover what's really going on.

From three different lawyers responding to the same brief, the client is most likely to choose the one who helps them sleep better at night – the one who eases their anxiety. How often do you meet lawyers who truly understand this and frame their proposal with the goal of providing that reassurance? Too often, you'll encounter lawyers who focus on impressing with their expertise – offering in-depth analysis of data, explaining the process, and diving into the risks and complexities of the case. But what clients really need is to feel reassured that everything will be taken care of and everything will be well.

Clients tend to stick to what they know – their industry norms or what's worked for them in the past. Sometimes, it takes a fresh pair of eyes – your eyes – to spot opportunities they've completely overlooked. Challenge their brief. Analyse a broader picture.

When Henry Ford decided to build the Model T, he wasn't just thinking about making a cheaper and better car. He was thinking about *transportation.* The real challenge was about *rethinking the whole game.*

Ford didn't sit around tweaking the old design and trying to upgrade it. No, he threw the playbook out of the window. He introduced

mass production. Suddenly, it wasn't about having a handful of experts make a handful of expensive cars – it was about **scaling** the whole process, cutting costs and making cars affordable.

Ford didn't just solve the problem. He *reinvented* the whole system. And that's what happens when you challenge the challenge. You don't just find a solution – you find a whole new way to think about the problem.

The electric car is a more recent example, when instead of following the traditional path of perfecting internal combustion engines to reduce emissions, a new, game-changing vehicle was created. Tesla challenged the entire car culture, the infrastructure and even our idea of what a car should do.

These are big and famous examples. But we come to similar unchallenged challenges all the time. 'We need to increase traffic to the website,' says the brief. But will it really lead to generating more leads or better conversion rates? What business objectives is the client trying to achieve by increasing the traffic? 'We want to improve our customer service skills.' Is the problem really the lack of skills or changed customer expectations? What do we know about the customers' journeys and experiences?

Challenging the challenge isn't about being difficult; it's about being thorough and strategic. By digging deeper, you not only find smarter solutions but also create real lasting value for your clients. It's not about rushing to answers – it's about making sure you're answering the right question.

If you do not have a formal brief from your prospective client you will have to rely even more on your conversation with them and all the intelligence you can gather.

First of all, have a proper Q&A session. Remember that you have to approach it as a journalist, not as a market researcher doing a questionnaire. Your role is not to ask questions and record the answers. Your role is to listen very carefully and get all the clues (verbal and non-verbal) to get the full story out of them. Watch the best interviewers – see how they are looking for the right end of the thread, then when they find it they start pulling, untying the whole knot. While everyone knows about the importance of storytelling, we often forget another very valuable skill – story-*listening*. You need to have your personal radar on for all clues, hints and mismatches in order to hear what is *not* being said, ask relevant questions and clarify the answers. If you work in a team, make sure that the person who reads the room best is with you at the meeting. It is also a good reason to choose people with different personality styles for such a meeting – they will notice different things and complement each other. The important thing is to remind everyone before the meeting why you are doing it: to build connection and hear the true story. If your 'story-listening meeting' (Q&A session) goes well, you have already pre-sold your product, whatever it might be.

Helpful tools

Simple tools like SWOT analysis (Strengths, Weaknesses, Opportunities, Threats) and the PECSTEL framework (Politics, Economics, Customer, Socio-demographics, Technology, Environment and Legislation) can be effective ways to explore problems.

PECSTEL can be used for scenario planning and horizon scanning and is excellent for understanding the context of problems. Here's what the initials stand for:

Politics – what's going on internally within the organisation (especially at board level) and externally in the country or internationally which will affect the company, its products, services and performance?

Economics – how is the macro-economic situation impacting on the company or industry's ability to trade? What are stock prices doing in the sector? What are the supply chain issues? What is the cost of debt?

What investments are being made? What taxes or tariffs will affect the company and how?

Customer/Competition – what behaviours are consumers/customers exhibiting? How are the competitors operating? What trends are emerging in the industry you're pitching?

Socio-demographics – what population changes will affect the market? For example, during Covid, the dispersal of many people to rural locations and out of cities had a huge impact on consumer goods companies' distribution costs and reduced their profitability. What are societal or generational changes doing to the market you are looking at in your pitch?

Technology – new innovations such as AI and quantum computing can enable disruptive players to enter markets and can also kill established players if they don't adapt quickly enough. The established automotive manufacturers laughed in 2018 when Elon Musk said he wanted Tesla to be the biggest car manufacturer in the world. They're not laughing any more. What is technology enabling or inhibiting in the case of the pitch you're working on?

Environment/Ethics – the world is now torn between governments that prioritise green policies and those who 'drill, baby, drill' and want access to cheap, polluting energy sources. Some consumers care about the ethics of the companies they support; others focus on day-to-day practicalities and affordability. What are the dynamics at play in the pitch you are making? For example, there are many venture capitalists now who look for a social or ethical component in the investments they make – who want their investments to have a social purpose as well as a commercial proposition. You need to know who you are playing to and what values they think are important; what are those values and what do they mean for your pitch?

Legislation – what laws are going through the statute books in Washington, Brussels, Beijing and other local or international centres of power which will have consequences for your client or the people you are pitching to? Small changes in legalities – even in other countries – can have big ramifications for industries. What's on the legislative agenda? What policies are governments and candidates advocating which will affect your market or the people you are pitching to?

CHAPTER 10
Product

'People don't know what they want until you show it to them'
STEVE JOBS

If you have done everything described above then this stage should be relatively easy. You now have to link your solution to their requirement and convince them that your product solves the problem. This is the time when you might need to go outside your pitching team and use other resources too.

Use the best brains in your company

You may need some 'grey-hairs'. They have experience. They have seen many problems before. But do not be driven by them. Challenge and analyse every 'been there, done that' statement they make. While it's useful to get the perspective of people who have witnessed the type of problem you're facing before, beware of the 'curse of the expert'. Experts and grey-hairs may speed up your diagnosis and come up with quick solutions, but their solutions are also likely to be based on what's worked in the past.

You should invite any bright sparks you know, irrespective of their age, seniority or expertise, to meet with the pitch team and share their views. Invite someone from a different team. People with fresh eyes that are unbound by the conventions of the market or industry may come up with novel ideas or perspectives. They may see an angle no one else will. They'll have the 'objectivity of ignorance' on the client's business. Occasionally, fresh eyes spot possibilities that those too involved or too 'native' cannot see.

As we said before, your pitch is about the promise. Your solution (product) may change, but at the moment you have to convince yourself to be able to convince your client that it is the best one. There are lots of tools available to help you do this. We prefer the ones below.

Six Thinking Hats

With plaudits to Edward de Bono (the father of the term 'lateral thinking'), this is a technique that helps you deconstruct the client's issues so that you can tackle the problem from specific angles rather than as one indigestible whole. These six distinct perspectives are represented metaphorically by coloured hats.

The team puts on six different coloured hats, in sequence:

White hat for facts and data. What do we *know* from the information we have? What do we need to find out?

Red hat for emotions and feelings. What do we *feel* about this issue and about the client? What does my gut instinct have to say about this? This is about your intuition, not about facts or logic.

Black hat for pessimism. Examine the weaknesses. What's the worst that can happen? What are the contingency plans? What risks are attached to the problem and our product/solution?

Yellow hat for optimism. Look for benefits, opportunities and feasibility. What can be gained from implementing our recommendation? What will be the upsides?

Green hat for freshness. What completely new insights do we have? What lateral thoughts and ideas can be brought to bear?

Blue hat for sky – the overview. Bring the other elements together – all the other thoughts and ideas produced from the previous coloured-hat discussions – and sift through them to produce an overall picture. The synthesis will be your solution template.

This systematic approach ensures diverse perspectives. It may not produce the exact right answer but you will have a robust discussion and a thorough analysis of different aspects of your solution. It's particularly effective for group discussions and evaluation of complex problems.

A logic chain

All your thoughts and ideas need to be condensed and ordered. A truly useful tool is the logic chain. This is a single sheet of paper on which the skeleton of your overall argument is written. It is a series of sequential statements that:

- Articulate the client's central issue
- List the core reasons for this situation
- Describe the desired outcome
- Describe your hypothesis for remedy and your reasons for this remedy
- Anticipate the results of taking this action
- Articulate how it will be measured for effectiveness.

All through the pitch period, the logic chain acts as your guide. It will change over the course of your investigation, as your thinking develops and as you discover new information about your client, investor or task. Once it is as good as you can make it, you will hang your presentation around it. Keep coming back to it to test that it is clear and compelling and relevant in the light of any new information. It's also useful because it will help you explain your case quickly.

Any winning pitch must be boiled down to a simple case that can be articulated quickly. Some of the best are made in five minutes or less, for example:

- Abraham Lincoln's Gettysburg Address, which redefined the meaning of the American Civil War to be a conflict about the ideals

of liberty and equality, was only 272 words long and delivered in just two minutes. It changed history.
- Francis Crick and James Watson, the Cambridge geniuses who discovered DNA, described it in a five-minute pitch to win the Nobel prize.
- The pitch to Hollywood producers for the film *Alien* was 'Jaws ... in space'.

As pitch consultants we are often asked to edit presentations. We have helped entrepreneurs on the London Business School *Launchpad* programme pitch their business ideas to venture capitalists. We get them to focus single-mindedly on what we know VC investors prioritise – the go-to-market strategy, a differentiated product, a credible team and a good articulation of the problem that the product or service solves. They have to deliver all this in just four minutes.

A good logic chain gives you a better chance of distilling your work into something that people will actually want to listen to. Another speaker at Gettysburg spoke for two hours. No one remembers him or his pitch.

Test your hypotheses

Use the time you have to try out your ideas and test your logic on a number of stakeholders to help you mould your thinking. These include dispassionate colleagues, focus groups, third-party individuals with specific expertise and, of course, the clients. Do anything you can to torture-test your viewpoint. Not just for logic and technical merit, but also for how it will play with the client.

Other tools you can use for aligning your product with the client's needs include the Value Proposition Canvas and the FAB.

The Value Proposition Canvas

This framework breaks down the client's needs into three categories:

Gains, **Pains** and **Jobs-to-be-done**. You then map your product's features to address those categories.

- **Gains:** What positive outcomes is the client hoping for?
- **Pains:** What challenges, obstacles or frustrations are they facing?
- **Jobs-to-be-done:** What are the key tasks they need to accomplish?

Your pitch should show how your product delivers on each of these areas – how it eases their pains, delivers the gains they're looking for, and helps them accomplish their key jobs.

The 'FAB' (Features, Advantages, Benefits) Method

This classic technique is designed to break down the product in a way that helps the client understand exactly how it meets their needs.

- **Features:** What is your product? What does it do?
- **Advantages:** Why is your product the best choice? What makes it stand out from other options?
- **Benefits:** How does this product solve the client's problem or improve their situation? This is where you tie the product back to their specific needs.

CHAPTER 11

Profit

By 'profit' we mean several aspects of pitching. If the pitch is successful and, as a result, a deal is made, both parties should profit from this agreement. Figuring out this profit right from the start is a big and important part of working on a pitch. Sadly, this is very often seen as a separate exercise. (It comes from the 'don't worry about the money now' school of new business.)

The team may sometimes find out the client's budget or estimate their project price. They may plan resources needed for pitching. Yet companies rarely approach this question systematically. So they lose the pitch not because the price is too high but because they haven't made the price relevant to the decision. They work on assumptions, estimates and guesses, and fail to demonstrate value. 'We are too expensive for them' is the most common explanation we hear after a lost pitch. More often than not, this isn't the real reason, it's just an excuse.

To make sure that your pricing strategy is relevant and that this important part of the client's decision goes as smoothly as possible, you have to start talking about money at the earliest stages of your pitch. This does not mean you open the first conversation with a questionnaire on money. However, you should not be shy about talking about the financial side of the business and the value of the project either. After all, you must both benefit from working with each other!

You need to understand the client's process for financial planning, their principles, issues, criteria, who signs off their budget and how it is done, how they involve procurement or any third parties and what they value most. If you don't understand all this, it will come back to bite you. This can happen in a variety of ways, some of which might surprise you.

A consultancy we know pitched for a very large project which would reshape the client's company worldwide. It would impact the way they looked, the way they behaved, it would require retraining thousands of staff on the new company story. It meant communicating to the City, investor audiences and shareholders the rhyme and reason for this huge change. Customers would have to be convinced that the company they loved was the same but different. The job would take months to complete, involve multiple stakeholder consultations, numerous reports, wide-ranging fieldwork, the production of materials in several languages and large-scale events all over the world to launch the new identity and company value proposition.

When the consultancy presented their price for doing this job, it made the client worry. But not for the reason you may suppose. It was way cheaper than all the other consultancies they had asked to pitch. So the client got alarmed that this consultancy had not understood the nature of the task and was ill-equipped to execute the assignment. By being too cheap, they had created doubt in the client's mind. They had to work hard to undo that damage.

If the consultancy had begun to seed the conversation about price expectation much earlier, they would have avoided this situation. By assuming they had to undercut, they misjudged the client's perceptions and nearly lost the job.

More often, price becomes a barrier because it is perceived as too high. This can be headed off at the pass by making sure you get to the right decision-makers. Most tend to focus on the *specifier* buyer – the one who needs the work done. And we neglect to engage with the *economic* buyer – the one who signs the cheques. It is always worth taking the trouble to run a parallel process with the economic buyer alongside the specifier buyer in a pitch. People such as the chief financial officer, the financial controller and the procurement officer are also your clients and have a vested interest in getting the right solution and partner. Start getting to know the CFO and their team and the procurement people in order to understand their priorities, planning cycle and budgetary sign-off procedures. We always get early dialogue with these people at proposal stage so there are no nasty surprises towards the end of the pitch process. If you get them on board, it makes the process much smoother.

Additionally, there are techniques that help you to *contextualise* your proposed price. Many pitchers leap straight from the problem to the solution and attach a price tag for providing that solution. More often than not, this price encounters opposition. Why? Because a vital stage has been left out of the dialogue.

You must always contextualise your price. Not by relating it to the amount of work you will need to do but, for example, by helping the client to understand the *real* cost of doing nothing, of letting the situation continue unresolved. If you work in the world of business development and sales, you might be asked to help organisations get better at pitching. We could say, 'We run a programme which skills up your people on pitching technique and a "pitch doctor" programme on a live assignment to coach your teams to win. The cost for both of these over a six-month period is £100,000.'

We're going to get a 'no'. A hundred grand is a lot of investment.

However, if we lead the client through a price contextualisation process, we will have a different outcome.

Q: 'How many pitches do you run a year?'
A: 'About 20.'
Q: 'And what's a good client worth?'
A: 'A decent client is £150k per year.'
Q: 'How many pitches do you win?'
A: 'Roughly 40 per cent.'
'Okay, let me see if I've got this right. You're pitching for £3 million

worth of business each year, but you're only winning £1.2m. That means you're leaving £1.8 million on the table. And that's without counting the hidden costs – staff time, lost opportunities, distractions from existing clients. That's another £500k, maybe more. You're looking at a £2–2.5 million problem.

'Let's look at the upside if we improve that situation: if you got to a 50 per cent conversion rate – winning ten out of the twenty pitches instead of just eight – that would add another £300,000 of income. And if you got to 70 per cent conversion, you'd win another £900k of income. What sort of difference would that make to your company's financial performance?'

When you've taken the client through the consequences of underperforming, you've contextualised your £100,000 proposal to solve a £2m–2.5m problem. You could then discuss the situation in other key markets and see if the problem is even bigger.

Work out this exercise for what you do. Can you contextualise the case for the client investing in your solution? Can you monetise the cost of doing nothing and the opportunity of producing better commercial results? If you can, it'll make the fee for working with you seem outstandingly good value.

Nowadays, nearly all companies that offer professional services experience tough negotiations with client procurement departments. Don't be fazed. Hold your nerve. Remember, they want your services and your team – otherwise they would not be having this conversation with you. Procurement teams are also human. They just have a job different from yours. Their task is to approach your project from a different perspective – *to obtain it with care and effort.*

Whereas it may seem to you that all they want is to lower costs, their real objective is to optimise value, cost, quality and risk. And it is your job to remind and assure them of the value and quality and to mitigate any risk. Your fees must obviously be in the competitive range, but however you arrive at your financial proposal – time-based, commission, cost plus, value-based – you have to present your fees as true value for money and to show them to be cost-effective for your client.

To be able to do it you need to take into account different scenarios and considerations. If you leave this until after the presentation, you will likely lose. We have heard people say, 'We won the pitch but lost at the negotiation stage.' This is a mistake. People lose when they do not spend enough time with the client, to listen and understand what the client really needs. Clients are human. If they see something they like, they want to get it at an affordable price.

We have to listen to clients really well to understand what 'affordable' means for them. They may be interested in a long-term partnership and will be able to pay a premium if you share their risks. They may need more flexibility with payments or more transparency. Depending on your situation and your own objectives, you can work out several pricing strategies and models to offer to your client. So when they ask 'How much?' you are fully prepared.

You need to rehearse not only your 'solution' presentation, but also your fee presentation.

Here's an example of being properly prepared. When the procurement process hit our industry, advertising, many were scared. They didn't know how to take on these 'bean counters' who had been trained in negotiation, so they ran away. The enlightened ones, however, embraced procurement. They walked the procurement team through the processes involved with producing ads. Many procurement people move around their company's purchasing function – buying raw materials one day, manufactured components another and professional services the next. To buy efficiently they need to understand the economics of each function. By educating the procurement team, answering their questions and taking them inside our operation, we ensured that both parties had the same basis for calculations. There was no more comparing apples with pears. This resulted in mutually beneficial agreements and deals that considered other factors in addition to price, such as payment terms, cashflow, location of meetings, limits of requests for rework, a time bank of goodwill for the client to use when needed, reciprocal education investments to help both parties understand each other's pressures, and long-term incentives to reward with additional work.

Finally, what do you do if the other party is playing hardball? Stay calm. We know an attorney who specialises in employment law. He was commissioned by his client's general counsel to represent them in a discrimination case that had been brought by four ex-employees against the firm. At the end of the meeting, the general counsel said: 'Oh, by the way, I need you to go down the corridor to our procurement director's office just to dot the i's and cross the t's on our contract.'

The attorney duly walked down the corridor and knocked on the door of the PD's office.

'Come!' came the command from inside.

Our lawyer friend went in.

'Sit!' barked the PD, pointing at the chair in front of his desk, without looking up from his desk.

The lawyer sat and started taking his papers out of his briefcase.

Still without looking up, the PD ordered: 'Before you even think of taking your papers out of your case, I want your agreement to a minimum 15 per cent discount on your hourly rate if we allow you to handle this case on our behalf.'

Our friend started putting his papers back in his case. He fastened the clasp and stood up, making to leave. For the first time, the procurement director looked up at him.

'Where are you going?' he enquired.

'I'm so sorry,' the lawyer said, 'I totally misunderstood what this meeting was about. I now realise it's about getting a few quid off my hourly rate whereas I originally thought it was about me stopping your firm from losing four cases of discrimination, each one of which carries a financial penalty of unlimited liability if you lose, which will most likely cost the company at least £1 million per plaintiff. My mistake.'

He moved to the door.

Realising that his bluff had been called, the procurement director, who had been briefed to hire this specific lawyer, said: 'Please, sit back down. I am sure we can reach an agreement.'

They could. The lawyer's full hourly rate.

Don't be bullied. Don't be a supplicant. Meet as equals. You both have something the other party wants. Conversations about profit are all a matter of perception and helping the other party feel seen, heard and understood. When that happens, you can have a peer-to-peer conversation and move towards agreement. Remember: your objective is to give the other party what they want but on terms that are acceptable to you.

If you need more help in planning for this particular element of the pitch process, check out *The Work Smarter Guide to Negotiation*.

CHECKLIST

Process
- [ ] Have a 'Pitch Playbook' specifically developed for your company.
- [ ] Decide which tools (including AI tools) you are going to use.
- [ ] Get to know the client's processes.
- [ ] Get to know the client's criteria for deciding the winner.
- [ ] Adjust the format of your meetings to the pitching format – online or offline.
- [ ] Book at least three rehearsals in everyone's diaries.

Promise
- [ ] Formulate your main ideas as an exciting promise of a better future.
- [ ] Prepare and rehearse your introduction: link people's stories with their roles for clients.
- [ ] Demonstrate your personal interest in the project, don't just say it.

Problem
- [ ] Read the brief carefully – check every detail.
- [ ] Clarify the brief (especially abstract words like 'transformation', 'creative solution', 'cultural change' and so on) – get to know what the client means exactly.
- [ ] Read between the lines – understand:
    - Cultural context: company culture and national culture if relevant
    - Historical context: the history of the problem
    - Situational context: the present situation and the client's current challenges.
- [ ] Challenge the challenge:
    - Do they say what they really need or just what they want?

– Can you look at the problem from a new perspective or frame it differently?

Product

- [ ] Use the best brains in your company; go outside the team.
- [ ] Use several different tools to test and debate your ideas (Six Thinking Hats, for example).
- [ ] Test your idea/hypothesis on colleagues, focus groups or neutral third-party individuals.

Profit

- [ ] Start to talk about the money early – understand the client's mindset, process and decision-making specifics.
- [ ] Get to know the economic buyers and engage them in the conversation from the first stages of the pitch preparation.
- [ ] Contextualise your price – relate it to the size of the problem and demonstrate the value you are creating.
- [ ] Thoroughly rehearse your fee presentation as well as your presentation of the solution.
- [ ] Anticipate questions and get your answers ready.
- [ ] Meet as equals. You cannot propose a partnership of equals when you are on bended knee.

PART IV

PRESENTING YOUR PITCH

'I think you can be a good comedian with jokes you're doing on the first try. But you can't be a great comedian without editing and reworking'

JERRY SEINFELD, WORLD'S RICHEST COMEDIAN

CHAPTER 12
It's showtime!

You've run an exemplary process. Now it's time for the show.

What is the most important thing about the show? It is not about what you say. It's about *how* you say it.

The same story can be told many times in many different ways – films and theatre productions provide numerous examples of how the same script can create a moving and memorable performance or a flop. There have been legendarily famous productions of *Hamlet*, just as there have been ignominious ones that have sunk without trace. Shakespeare's script is the same; it's how it's played that differentiates the experience.

It's the same with your pitch presentation. The thinking and the text may be logical, incisive and brilliant. But you have to *play it* well. Persuasion happens between the people in the room – not on the slides of your presentation deck. So many people, making presentations all over the world every day, forget this truth. They rush to write the deck and pour effort into the charts, the graphs and the bullet points. They think this is the job. They are wrong. If it was simply about writing your iron-clad case down on slides, you could email the presentation deck to the client.

We've all experienced shows where people forget to breathe when the drama is unfolding in front of their eyes. Where the audience laugh, or cry, or do both and applaud at the end. If we can make a room full of tough US household-goods manufacturers weep over what it means for Indonesians to live mosquito-free, you can move your audience with your stories, too.

What do the best presenters do that differentiates them from the rest?

It is *you* who breathes life into mere words

Start with yourself. To be convincing you have to be convinced yourself. As we said before, people buy *conviction*. Your conviction. They want certainty and fluency.

You have to believe in your product, your idea, the solution you've come up with. If you have doubts or think your competitor's offer is superior or that your price is too high, or if you don't believe your organisation has the right credentials, it will show.

Conviction is very convincing. It's tangible. You can *feel* it. The weight of your own belief, the conviction carried in the words you speak, the urgency of your body's posture, the energy in your voice all convey to your audience the veracity of what you are communicating to them. If you *genuinely* believe what you are pitching is brilliant – the most amazing product, the funniest script or yourself for a new job – you are halfway there.

Everything in pitch presentations starts and ends with you, not the charts.

Rules of the show and how to break some

We see a lot of presentations. We coach a lot of presenters – younger, older, non-native speakers, analytical people, introverts, extroverts, blaggers, the nervous, show-offs, the timid, the courageous. Every single one of them can communicate clearly and with conviction with the right preparation, guidance and practice.

To play your part of the show well, you need to know the rules. But real 'rules' often get confused with habits. Or assumptions. Or 'the way it's always been done around here'. There are certain things that people always expect from a presentation:

- Structure
- Adherence to time restrictions
- Appropriate people in the meeting

- Knowledge of the material
- Ability to answer questions

In addition to these common-sense rules, there may also be specific rules laid down by the people you are presenting to for how they wish to conduct all the pitches. And on top of all that, we often impose our own stylistic habits and conventions:

- Go round the room with 'name, rank, number' standard introductions (what we call 'the creeping death')
- Trot out our credentials
- Regurgitate the brief
- Regurgitate the objectives
- Show them all the hard work we've done to get to the answer
- Take them through some case studies

None of these are sacred rules carved in stone. If you play by all of those conventions, you think you are playing safe. In fact, it's the opposite: the riskiest thing you can do is to be forgettable and sound like everyone else – to obey the 'rules' of standard pitch presentations. In a world of cookie-cutter pitches, boldness stands out. Breaking a convention says, 'I'm different. I lead, I never follow.'

To make your presentation effective you often have to break some rules. Break the wrong rule and you look careless. Break *the right rule* and you're unforgettable.

Your audience is expecting a long preamble, charts, stats, the usual routine – a standard pitch presentation. Instead, you cut to the chase and tell them everything you're going to tell them over the next forty-five minutes up front, in one minute.

Or you start with a story. Something personal. Maybe even funny. (We know someone in mergers and acquisitions who always starts by saying 'We're a bit weird.' It's intriguing.)

Or you ask them a question.

Or you make a bold and contentious statement.

Or you engage them in a quick game.

We know someone who was pitching to a chemical company on the need to train their senior executives on crisis PR management in the media. She started her pitch by placing a bowl of water with a goldfish in it on the centre of the table.

> *This water is from the outflow pipe at one of your plants which drains into the local river system. It is so full of untreated pollutants that by the time this presentation is over, this goldfish will have died. So what my listeners on BBC Radio 4's* Today *programme want to know is this: as the board in charge of this company, how can you look at yourselves in the mirror every morning?*

She then placed a microphone on the table in front of the board with a green light which read 'ON AIR'.

It worked.

On a different occasion we were brought in to get the leadership team of a large tech company to align. They were briefing against each other inside the company, forming cliques and generally not pulling in the same direction. They all held shares. We opened our pitch by saying we wanted to catch a news bulletin on Sky. It was actually a short pre-recorded video clip we'd shot in a studio the day before:

> *Reports are coming in to our City desk this morning that three directors from the unicorn fashion-tech company XYZ have resigned as a result of a major bust-up in the boardroom. Rumours of disagreements amongst the leadership team have been rumbling for weeks but today those rumblings erupted into resignation and rancour. Since trading opened*

only an hour ago, 20 per cent of the company's value has been wiped out. Here's our business editor, Sophie Dexter, with the latest. Sophie...

The people in the conference room had walked in with other things on their minds, expecting a bog standard 'team-building' session (yawn). We had their attention now.

You've immediately triggered the neurotransmitters that signal 'Threat! I need to focus on this.'

There's real power in breaking the mould.

How do you know which rule you should break? Ask yourself about every single rule or convention:

- Does this rule help me and my audience to build better understanding?
- Does it pull my audience closer?
- Does it help me to communicate the message or does it exist merely for convenience?
- Does it make me more real, more human?

For example, the rule that says everyone is supposed to hold back their questions till the end. It's tidy. It's predictable. It lets you say what you want to say. But if you engage your audience and encourage them to jump in whenever they want, you can turn the whole presentation into a conversation. Now they're part of it, not just spectators. And you'll focus on the areas your audience find of most interest.

Think what specifically you would like to communicate about you and your team. Thoroughness? Personal touch? Speed? Creativity? Care? Demonstrate it in the way you deal with rules and the expectations of your prospective clients or partners. Find a way to produce the impression and to be in control of your pitch delivery.

Other ways to differentiate yourself

One of the first things to consider is timings and deadlines. Clients often expect you to deliver a written document to their Request for Proposals (RFP) by a certain date. Go beyond what they expect from you and beat that deadline. Deliver it three days ahead of time. And, apart from an email version, deliver your response by hand to the person in charge – printed or in another format. This is one of the immediate goals we set for anyone whom we are advising when we act as 'pitch doctors'. Firstly, it's a shock to most companies who are used to doing everything right up to the wire – it's a signal that, this time, the pitch is going to be done differently. Secondly, it's one of the first opportunities you get to differentiate yourself from the competition with the client. Delivering early is a statement of intent and demonstrates that you do not produce documents at the last minute.

We want to create a positive impression in every interaction we have with our clients; this is usually an easy one that kicks off the whole process.

CHAPTER 13
Control everything you can

Breaking presentation rules does not mean creating chaos. It means careful and meticulous staging of your presentation and controlling everything you can. Planning for failure, having 'healthy' paranoia, thinking, *What could go wrong?*

We've experienced the following nightmares:

- Builders turning on a pneumatic drill beneath our presentation room just as we stood up to begin our presentation.
- Office cleaners coming in at night and putting all the presentation boards from our highly confidential pitch out on the street for the refuse collectors in the morning. To add insult to injury, some of the larger pieces had been turned into shelters from the rain by the local homeless community.
- A colleague made his bit of the presentation and then, satisfied he'd been brilliant, swung round in his swivel chair while we carried on with the rest of the show. The client noticed and didn't appoint us because we 'didn't appear to be a close team'. Too right we weren't.
- The clients came into our reception for the presentation and there, right in front of them, was that morning's edition of an industry magazine emblazoned with a six-inch-high headline saying we'd lost our biggest client.
- The clients asked if we could leave them alone in the presentation suite for a few minutes. We vacated the room. During their discussion they walked around the room and spotted the notes we'd been writing to each other as the meeting progressed. They weren't impressed

when they read: 'the w****r in the glasses looks like trouble'. We didn't win that one.

Check if the local authority has scheduled to dig up the road on the day you're presenting. (If they have, move location or persuade them to stop for an hour.) Make sure you lock away your confidential materials. Practise behaving like a team and listening to each other supportively – not just presenting your bit and then mentally checking out. Manage the environment so you look at your best, whether playing at home or away or online. Notice *everything*. And don't say or write down derogatory things about what's going on – either in a private chat or on notepads. (*Manners makyth man*, as the school motto goes.)

Don't leave it to fate, to whim or to others. You should be in full control of:

- The team who will present
- Where you go in the order of presenting
- Timing
- Location
- Room setup and environment
- Technology
- Backups (e.g. the appropriate plug adaptors for pitches in other countries)
- Logistics (pick-up times, overnight accommodation)
- Dress code

Presenting team

This is, probably, the most difficult thing to do, but it is important that you should weed out those who can damage your presentation. Even if it's your CEO who refuses to rehearse.

So find the best presenters. Presenting abilities and skills do not always correspond with titles and seniority levels. The American comedian Steve Martin once said, 'Some people have a way with words. Other people, not have way.'

People who 'not have way' do not get to present. It's too important. You get one crack at this; you cannot afford weak presenters. It's difficult to be ruthless. We want to be nice to people. But we must be ruthless because no one will be happy or thank us for losing the pitch.

If you are pitching a team project, you need to demonstrate that you work as a team, not as a group of individual experts. Clients want bright people who spark off each other, who respect each other and who clearly get excited working together. That's called chemistry. It's the magic that happens when the whole is greater than the sum of its parts. And it's exciting when you feel it. The pitch audience must feel the chemistry between your team members. They must also feel the chemistry between your team and them.

Your pitch presentation is designed to sell your idea by making the clients fall in love with your team. People want to hire people with whom they will enjoy working. You need to infect your audience with your team's enthusiasm and conviction. It's not just serendipity. It needs to be cultivated deliberately and practised.

In order to look like a team, there are specific things you can do in your presentation that will signal togetherness. For example: make the handovers between speakers interesting and smooth. Here is the standard way: 'I will now hand over to my colleague, Maria, who will talk you through our strategic recommendations.' Maria shuffles her papers together and gets to her feet to start her bit of the presentation.

How much better is it to rehearse a handover that's slicker and looks spontaneous? For example: 'We conducted six research groups. Two in Scandinavia, one in France, and three in South East Asia. At the groups we found three very interesting types of reaction to your service. In South East Asia ... well, Maria, you were in the group in Singapore. Tell us what happened.' Maria, who knew this was coming, because you had rehearsed it together, immediately kicks in with her comments.

'Yes, Tanya, what we found in Singapore was totally different from other markets and it got us thinking ...'

Doesn't sound like much, does it? But it signals teamwork and fluency and, crucially, picks up the pace of the narrative so it feels like you're listening to a story, not a formal presentation.

The order of presenting

It does matter if you present first, last or somewhere in the middle. People very often overlook this very important detail. However, it is important to find out as early as possible when you are presenting – if you can influence it, do so. (Remember, seek to influence anything that you can.) Are you and your competitors presenting on different days? Then definitely ask to present last. Normally clients are only too happy to oblige. Going last has several competitive advantages:

- You will get more time to prepare and rehearse your pitch.
- You will be the last team they'll see and so benefit from 'recency' – their memory of you will be fresher.
- Most crucially, you can get to the important stuff quicker. By now they will have been subjected to several pitch presentations, with all the research analysis, task regurgitation and other non-value-added guff. You do not need to do this; you can get to the answers they are waiting for much faster while you still have their full attention.

If you are presenting one after another on the same day, it may also be to your advantage to present last if all the presentations are short and don't finish late in the day. If it is going to be a long day for your client, then you are probably better off going first.

The lunch break is another important moment to take into account. Are you presenting just before lunch or immediately after? These are, probably, the worst possible time slots for pitch presentations. You have to be aware of it and creative with managing energy in the room.

There is no one definite prescription for the order of presenting. The most important thing is that you think about it as early as possible. Then you can either try and change the time or, if that's not possible, mitigate the negative effects of being in a bad time slot.

You need to look at it not only from the point of view of your presentation logic but also from the client's viewpoint. If they are tired and their energy is low by the time it is your turn to enter the room, you need to wake them up. We often get them up on their feet to do something physical.

We use the activity as a metaphor for what we are about to present. It might be, for example, that we get them to raise their arm and move it round to the right as far as they can and to notice where they get their arm to. We then ask them to close their eyes, do the same exercise in their imagination and move their arm way, way beyond where they got it to on the first try. Then they open their eyes, raise their arm for a second time and move it round to the right as far as they can again. Without fail, everyone's arm travels another 20 per cent further than it did on the first attempt.

So what?

So, we explain, we're here today to help them:

- Go beyond what they thought they were capable of.
- Rewire their employees' mindsets to work differently.
- Get more out of their resources (money, time, people) than they thought possible, just through seeing the world slightly differently.

Make your own link. It's powerful.

Either control your position in the running order or turn it to your advantage, even if you have the graveyard slot.

Timing

There is a great difference between presenting your pitch in five minutes and in forty-five. Usually, you plan and prepare your presentation to a specific time limit. But life is life. Be prepared if things change dramatically at the last minute. Tanya was once in a pitch as an interpreter for the head of planning. It was a big international pitch and she spoke English much better than her boss. We knew that we had about twenty minutes to present the proposal for our country and it gave us enough time for the top guy to present and Tanya to do a simultaneous translation into beautiful English. The night before the presentation we found out that we would only have five minutes: no time to translate anything. The night was spent on rehearsing: now Tanya was presenting everything and the head of planning was just smiling and clicking the slides.

Be prepared in case the client demands you present just the important stuff in two minutes. Have your precis version ready. We once presented to the British newspaper the *Sun*. Our presentation was timed for thirty minutes. We were phoned fifteen minutes before the presentation and told we would have the editor for just two minutes to show him the work. We did. It was a test. He liked three ideas, used one to run as a promotion the next day and rejected four. We were appointed on the spot and told to report to the newsroom that afternoon. It was like that for four years.

The most important thing you have to understand about the timing of the presentation is that you are not managing time. You are managing the audience – their attention, their energy, their chemistry.

We have seen again and again how people think about the structure of their presentation in terms of logical flow and level of detail. Everyone counts the number of slides and considers whether they have enough time to say everything they want to say. And almost no one thinks about managing the audience's energy levels, attention or levels of engagement.

If it is a very short format, do not waste valuable seconds on verbal introductions. Introduce yourself and the team in a big visual way. Make a statement by the way you enter the room, the way you stand, dress, position yourself or appear on screen. Grab their attention from the very first seconds. It is not about the words you use – it is about the energy flow, the confidence you exude, the curiosity and expectations you create.

According to research popularised by psychologist Albert Mehrabian, words are responsible for only 7 per cent of the impact of your message. The rest goes to the voice (38 per cent) and body language (55 per cent). And this is just about you. Imagine how much the environment adds to it. How warm the room is, how much air is flowing, how many bodies are in the room, whether the lighting is dark or daylight, how much ambient noise there is.

Your pitch presentation is a show. Treat it as such, whether it's on a 'stage' live in the room or on 'TV' via Zoom or Teams. At the very beginning the curiosity of the audience is at its maximum. Use it. Do not switch it off with 'housekeeping' notes, hesitant pauses or conventional introductions.

If you only have five minutes, start with the key point. Develop a strong powerful headline with your key message. Just one. A single-minded message requiring a single-minded response. Make your point. Explain and give evidence. End with a strong close that resonates. These are your five minutes. (This is often all you get with venture capitalists.)

If you have fifteen minutes, or slightly more, you can allow yourself to tell a story, to build a drama. So set the stage first: establish the context, articulate the purpose. You do not have to deal with headlines and slogans now. You have time to tell a story and build suspense.

In this longer format you can make two or three logically linked points or look at the same idea from different angles. You have an opportunity to engage with the audience – questions, clarifications, confirmations. Ask for audience feedback or reflections. If the format and the context permit, play a game, demonstrate or illustrate.

Wrap up by reinforcing your main point and then close. Closing should always bring the pitch presentation to the next concrete step. Do not end vaguely ('Are there any questions?' is a classic). The audience needs to know precisely what we do next. If you propose marriage, your partner should immediately understand that the next thing they do is put the ring onto their finger or open a bottle of champagne to celebrate.

What if your pitch delivery is longer than thirty minutes? The first thing is to think about the drama of your interaction with the audience. You cannot transmit your presentation to people for an hour. In fact, you should aim to present for no more than twenty minutes. TED Talks – some of the best presentations on the planet – are always shorter than eighteen minutes. Because this format works best. Attention spans are not very long. Listening is a difficult job. It requires a lot of energy. If you need to speak for considerably more than fifteen minutes, you can probably introduce a short break or two – have questions, discussion, show video clips, use illustrations or props to engage multiple senses. Never present for longer than thirty minutes without a break. Do not leave that break to chance. Plan it, orchestrate it, manage it – rearrange the room, play a game, put people in mini discussion groups, do something interactive where everyone participates.

Room and environment

If you are lucky enough to be given the choice, pitch at home. Pitching on your own turf gives you the advantage of orchestrating the environment to the most minute detail. From the office door (even from the street) everything should be contributing positively to your pitch. Security, reception, elevators, conference rooms, people meeting and greeting, and 'buzzing' around – signalling a dynamic environment.

Everything is part of the show. Like in a Michelin-starred restaurant. The experience is not just the food. Oh no. From the moment you enter, you are cocooned in three-star excellence. Everything runs on rails. At Lasarte in Barcelona, David encountered eleven members of staff just on his way to the table! Each and every phase of the restaurant – the door opening to let you in, welcoming you by name, taking your coat, escorting you to the table, seating you, unfolding the napkin, giving you the menu, explaining the menu, taking your drinks order, providing the wine list – every single detail is thought through and executed by nominated staff who know their role and are ever vigilant for your slightest need, alert to your every gesture and anticipating what you want minutes before you know you want it. They are alive to you and their environment.

Beware of the fact that in our own offices we quickly go native and stop noticing things a newcomer will see. We become 'building blind' – desensitised to the image our office creates. Our offices are not just convenient and efficient places for people to work. They are part of our brand image; they communicate messages.

Visit Google and you are ushered into the antidote to grey, anodyne corporate environments. Colour greets you everywhere. There are spaces for play and cafés for collaboration alongside tidy meeting rooms where everyone clears up after themselves. These are modern environments modelled around university campuses and there are even children to be seen because the firm is family friendly. This isn't written in reception on some sterile, Perspex 'Our values' noticeboard. It's signalled by the presence of IKEA high chairs in the cafeteria.

Think about all this before your client arrives. Don't leave it to chance. Are you pitching on the day when the office is nearly empty as most people are working from home? Is your office busy and buzzing or very quiet? What will the client see and feel the first moment the lift doors open at your floor? As the saying goes, a theatre starts with a cloakroom. The experience of your show always starts when your client walks through the door. It is not just a start, it is a setup for what follows. It creates the mood and expectations of your audience. So it is *very* important. Make sure that everyone from the security guy to the CEO is aware who you are hosting on the day and get them all onside.

In the second chapter, we talked about not losing. Not losing by avoidable mistakes. If your visitor is PepsiCo, don't have Coke on the refreshments tray. If you're hosting Apple, don't present from an HP laptop. Ensure the biscuits are *their* biscuits, the soap in the loos is *their* brand.

And if you're *re*pitching as the incumbent, don't suddenly paint a personal parking space for the client when they've already been a client for four years – they'll begrudge the last four years rather than think you've turned over a new leaf. And don't spend the first twenty minutes of your repitch reminding them of all the great things you've done for them over the last four years; they'll resent the history lesson and wonder why you aren't talking about the future – which is what pitches are supposed to be about.

If you are presenting at the client's office, go and see the room you'll be presenting in and work out how to use it best. Sketch out where all the electrical sockets are, the doors and windows. What kind of furniture does the room have? What kind of light? Where will you all sit? Does sound travel well? Will you need a microphone? Is there an IT person at hand? Can you get into the room earlier to set up? Remember, if anything can go wrong it will go wrong. Do not leave *anything* to chance.

You have to make sure that you and your team feel at home in that room, even if you are on the other side of the world. You want to feel confident and in control of your show. Being familiar with the environment calms down your reptile brain and allows you to focus on your client much better.

Be very attentive to how you behave to other people in the client's office. It is not only your office where you notice security guys, receptionists, tea ladies and other people making your life and work more enjoyable and comfortable. They may not be the key decision-makers on your pitch, but they notice you, your personal attitudes, your company culture. You may turn them into enemies or your greatest supporters. We know of many instances where a junior recruiter blocked a big 'name' in the industry from progressing through the job interview process because the 'big' person thought the junior recruiter wasn't important. Arrogance is never attractive.

Technology

We live in the twenty-first century. We depend massively on technology in business. Most of the time it works perfectly and we don't notice it. Sometimes we use the latest technology very deliberately to impress our audience. Definitely showcase your abilities with the most recent technological innovations if this is an important part of your image. But don't be a slave to technology. Remember, it's *you* people buy. Technology is only there to help you, not to substitute for you.

Technology, slides, visuals, props and other equipment are always double-edged swords. They are designed to help us communicate the message effectively and make our performance more engaging. On the other hand, when overused they steal the show. You must always be aware of where you want your audience's attention focused. Do you want them to stare at the screen or do you want eye contact? Are they buying your charts and your theories or you, your team and your capabilities? Are you in the room to build trust and relationships or to stare together at charts and bullet points? You know what we think.

Technology may fail you. Things just happen. You need to check and double-check that everything will work the way you planned it. And you need to have backups for the worst-case scenario. So, think about what you are going to do if:

- Your computer dies, gets stolen five minutes before the presentation, or (as happened to one of our colleagues) the client turns it off and says: 'Talk to me about how you can help my busines.'

- The Wi-Fi does not work.
- There is a major electricity cut in the building.
- There is an unannounced fire drill in the office right in the middle of your presentation. We had that situation once on a snowy February day. We reacted quickly, wrapped the clients in blankets, bought them hot drinks over the road and continued the pitch. They were impressed with how we didn't let this all faze us.

Will you have printouts? Will you sing and dance yourself if your video doesn't play? Do you have spare chargers, mobile Wi-Fi etc. ready?

In a word, are you ready to use your own smartness, take the steering wheel and the manual gear lever into your hands if your smart technology fails?

Q&A

First of all, prepare for it. Every pitch will prompt the audience to ask questions. (If they don't, you're in trouble – it means that nothing you said piqued their curiosity or made them think.) Start by trying to anticipate the questions they might ask. Ideally, think of the nastiest question they could ask. And then the second nastiest.

Clients inhabit their own world. Their picture of what you do will be far more wide-ranging than you might have anticipated. So be prepared for some quite esoteric lines of enquiry. Often, we anticipate questions about *us*. But they will be much more interested in getting into the nitty gritty about how you can help *them*. So they might ask you about their business rather than your specialism and also about details:

- Areas of expertise they think are vital but where you might be light or haven't mentioned because you've over-indexed in other areas. For

example, they might want expertise in tech when you've focused on investor relations.
- How you can mesh with their other partners/suppliers to save time and cost.
- Whether you can supplement their own in-house skills or even manage them.
- Market access across all their geographies.
- Regulatory knowledge in highly controlled markets and industries.
- Additional services you can provide which aren't in their original spec.

Brainstorm all possible questions and scenarios. Rehearse your answers. However, when you have rehearsed your answers do not plunge into answering as soon as you hear the first words of the question. Hear the client out. A Q&A session is as much about them having a chance to ask you as about your opportunity to answer them. It's a dialogue.

When you deliver your pitch you need to have a person in your team whose task is to listen and to watch. To listen and watch you and the audience. To read the room, the reactions. (If you are presenting solo you will have to do both at once.) It is a special skill and usually takes many years of practice. So if you are lucky enough to present as a team, choose one of you to be the main listener/observer. Take clues from this person when you open the dialogue with the client. The questions the client asks give you a wealth of intelligence. Starting with our school years when teachers and parents repeat the mantra 'read the question', we fail our exams again and again because we don't heed this advice. As adults, we still sometimes fail to read the intent behind the question.

Answering the question correctly starts with understanding the question. Not assuming, not guessing, but really understanding what is being asked and why. You must hear what they are saying and what they are *not* saying. What's being communicated between the lines? What are they revealing in their question about their concerns, expectations, hopes? What is on their agenda? Because when they ask their questions, they have their own agenda in mind. So listen carefully and actively, and clarify if you need to. What they're really saying may not even come in the form of a question. Remember the story about the senior executive at UPS saying what a shame it was that the CEO of the pitching company couldn't find time to visit WorldPort, their logistics hub? She wasn't saying it's a shame – she was saying, 'Go and visit it or you won't win our business.'

Allocate one person, or two people at most, to lead the answer on the questions you've anticipated. Everyone else shuts up. Otherwise you get carnage.

'What my colleague is trying to say ...' never goes over well. But if your answers aren't working, the pitch leader, who is in charge of the presentation meeting, must jump in and try to rescue the situation. (Don't leave colleagues twisting in the wind.) And if you get a curveball you hadn't anticipated, the pitch leader needs to buy time for the team to generate an answer. Something along the lines of: 'That's an interesting question. Just to make sure I've understood you, are you asking ... (restate the question)? What's the issue or concern behind that question?'

You can always answer in more detail after the presentation when you've had more time to think of a decent response. But if you just don't know, say so and offer to come back on the issue. Sincerity builds trust; bullshit dilutes it.

Finally, ask your own questions. It's a mistake that too many people make at all sorts of pitches – from job interviews to big international pitches. When asked 'Do you have any questions for us?', they regard it as a mere protocol of politeness and respond that everything is clear and they have no questions. What a waste of an opportunity to shine!

Questions are very important and powerful tools of

communication. Asking questions about the client, their business, their market, is an opportunity to demonstrate thoughtfulness, display knowledge and share insight. You can also use them to steer the conversation to your agenda and reveal your interests. In a word, with a good question you are not only finding out their story. You are telling yours.

Many pitch presentations are decided on the client's perception of how well you handle Q&A – not just answering questions (which tests your ability to exhibit grace under pressure), but also asking questions (to demonstrate your enthusiasm and that you've done your homework).

Think of the questions you want to ask. Make a long list – it should be long as you're curious and intelligent, remember? Select the best ones and ask them in priority order.

CHAPTER 14

Presenting a written pitch

> **Polonius: What do you read, my lord?**
> **Hamlet: Words, words, words.**
> WILLIAM SHAKESPEARE, *HAMLET*, ACT II SCENE II

We are surrounded by texts, bombarded with written words every single second of the day. These days, written content is created not just by writers and journalists, not just by humans but also by AI. As a result we are constantly exposed to many words but with very few *meanings* behind them.

'Reshape the future', 'facilitate and drive change', 'cultural transformation', 'competitive edge' – all of these clichés sound so familiar, so tempting to use and to hide behind. Many people describe what they or their companies do in these abstract terms. Do they create a true picture of what's on offer and build better understanding? Ask ten people working in the same company to give definitions, examples and associations that come into their head when they hear or read those words. How similar do you think they will be?

So do not treat your words like a school uniform – something designed to look neat and similar to others. Use your words for the purpose they were created: to express yourself. When writing your pitch, make sure it sounds human. 'Human' means individual, having personality, and being hand-made. It does not have to be perfect. But it does have to be clear and simple. Instead of abstract nouns, use words you can touch and feel, not just explain.

Use George Orwell's rules for language:

(i) Never use a metaphor, simile or other figure of speech which you are used to seeing in print. [For example, 'in a nutshell'.]
(ii) Never use a long word where a short one will do.
(iii) If it is possible to cut a word out, always cut it out.
(iv) Never use the passive voice where you can use the active voice.
(v) Never use a foreign phrase, a scientific word, or a jargon word if you can think of an everyday English equivalent.

Use everyday language. Write sharp, short sentences. Edit your work mercilessly – remove polysyllabic words and jargon; break long sentences into two or several. Jargon makes your text flat or, even worse, smacks of intellectual bullying. You've probably had that feeling if you've been to a novice lawyer or doctor and heard them use a lot of professional terms or Latin words. They may impress for a moment, but in the long term they annoy, sound pretentious and erode trust. Clarity builds understanding and trust. It is very hard to get a confident 'yes' from someone who is struggling to understand what you are talking about. All the words may be familiar (clichés are, by definition, very familiar to everyone) but if they do not form a clear, single-minded message, they remain just 'words, words, words'.

CHAPTER 15

Postscript

Listed below as a postscript are the most important things to remember when you are getting together your persuasive pitch presentation.

1. Rehearse, rehearse, rehearse

The minimum number of rehearsals is three. Not one. Not two. Three. Only after the third do you get any fluidity or coherence. Only after three do you create the chemistry that compels. It will be painful. No one likes doing it. Everyone will avoid actually rehearsing (they would rather talk through in vague terms: 'I'm going to say something like this ...' No, you're not; you're going to *say it*!). There will be tears, tempers and tantrums. Tough. Because rehearsals can be fraught with emotion (people feel emotionally exposed as their performance is critiqued), they are very good at uniting the team. The process of rehearsing is tough so it knits people together. You need them to knit together. That *esprit de corps* is infectious. And they will present much better as a result.

2. Presenters' energy

Here are some tricks to get your presenters' energy to the right level to perform. The body and voice need to be warmed up so the adrenaline coursing around your body is directed usefully. David has taken presenters who lacked conviction or the requisite energy to persuade off into a room, just the two of them for twenty minutes. When they come out, the level of delivery is tangibly, brilliantly better. What happens in the room? Those who have had this treatment never forget it. David gives them a tightly rolled-up newspaper – a thick one with plenty of pages. He has one too. Together, they smash the rolled-up newspaper with all their might onto the back of a chair ten times, very fast while counting out loud – 'one ... two ... three ...' – on every whack, up to ten. Then they throw the ragged newspaper into the air.

This exercise transforms your internal energy level and that gets reflected in the delivery of your pitch in the room or on screen. Some people don't like the idea of doing this exercise. They don't have the courage to try it and so they won't ever reap the rewards of extraordinary levels of presentational performance. Every single person who's done the exercise uses it from then on. Because it works.

3. Demonstrate what it means to you to win

We had to repitch to a financial client who we'd made famous as a brand. They meant a lot to our company and to us – financially, emotionally and reputationally. Before the final pitch presentation, we brought in a motivational speaker who revved us up and then got two members of our team to stand a metre apart and place a straight metal rod about half a centimetre thick between them – held between the softest part of their throats. On the count of three they walked towards one another holding each other's gaze. They bent the bar into a horseshoe shape. We held the bent bar up at the beginning of the presentation to tell the story and explained that this represented how we felt about re-winning this client. We won.

4. Mind your language

As a rule, most people speak too fast and fail to enunciate properly when they are presenting – both on screen and in real life. Rehearsal should help iron this out but beware: when you're presenting you need to slow down. Breathe. Speak up and project your voice. Emphasise the important points. Pause to let the significance of what you've just said land with the audience.

Before you go live, warm up your larynx by saying 'I WANT TO KICK YOU' five times out loud, enunciating every single syllable precisely.

S-L-O-W T-H-E H-E-L-L D-O-W-N.

CHECKLIST

- [ ] Make sure you and everyone in your pitching team are fully convinced. People buy conviction.
- [ ] Make a list of all the rules and conventions of pitching in your industry; identify what purpose each of them serves and which rules should be broken to make your pitch more effective.
- [ ] Think of ways to differentiate yourself in your presentation.
- [ ] Think of the image you want to create and the messages you want to convey; don't just say, demonstrate.
- [ ] Control everything you can:
    - Ensure the presenting team consists of the best presenters.
    - The order of presentation should work for you.
    - Adjust your presentation to the time available. Manage the audience within the overall timeframe.
    - The room and the environment should work for the benefit of your presentation.
    - Technology – check and double-check, have a plan B.
    - Q&A – prepare your answers and also the questions you want to ask; make this session part of your impact.
    - Manage your own energy and that of your client.
    - Use human language: simple, visual, personal.

PART V
POST-PITCH

'Many of life's failures are people who did not realise how close they were to success when they gave up'

THOMAS EDISON

CHAPTER 16
You have just left the room

No, you do not sigh with relief. It's not over yet. There's a lot more to be done to get over the finishing line. And the presentation isn't the finishing line for most pitch races.

There may be some pitches where you get an immediate answer. Some VCs may say yes (or no) immediately. TV production companies may buy the rights to your script idea at the end of the meeting. And when you go down on bended knee, it's rare you receive in reply, 'I'll think about it and give you the answer in due course.'

But in most business pitches – interviews, investment decisions, appointment of audit or legal advisors, manufacturing contracts and more – there's normally a timeline and a decision framework to allow the client to consider other options, consult, probe with further questions, negotiate and decide before they appoint.

The worst thing you can do now is relax. In Olympic sprints you do not stop at the finishing line if you want to win. Never. You keep running at full speed.

Gather the team together immediately. Reflect on the pitch, debrief on what happened and decide on the actions to take coming out of this discussion:

- Evaluate how the presentation went. What worked? What didn't land with the audience? What could have been done differently?
- What questions did they ask and how can you build on your initial response in more detail?

- What issues did they raise which you hadn't anticipated and need to respond to with a considered solution?
- What do you want to ask your 'mole', the person you've built the best relationship with at the client or intermediary?
- What else must you do to remain engaged and in dialogue?

This should be done minutes after you have left the room. Go to a nearby café and talk. Quickly decide what should be done in the next few hours. Impress your client with your speed, your teamwork and your responsiveness. Reassure them of your reliability with a thoughtful follow-up.

Sometimes you will not have done justice to your case during the presentation and you know there are doubts on the client side. Ask for immediate feedback from the person you've built the best relationship with at the client or intermediary (your 'mole'). Warts and all. Get their view. How did you do? What worked? What didn't? What are their doubts and what areas do you have to address?

Act on this feedback. Offer a face-to-face meeting between the main decision-maker and your CEO, to have a more intimate conversation, to discuss issues which may be confidential or sensitive, to build the connection at the highest level and to inspire confidence.

Do not give up; keep running.

Take and make action

1. Go through the questions they asked and work out what lay behind the questions. Look for themes or underlying issues, concerns or areas of interest.
2. Review the answers you gave in the meeting and work out if you addressed the concern or if more detailed follow-up is required (it is!).
3. Draw on your library of evidence to demonstrate efficacy and credibility in the areas you have identified are important to the clients in your follow-up. For example:

- Deep expertise within your team (this includes people who weren't in the pitch presentation) that is available to reassure the client of your credibility and resource.
- Relevant cases (written to be bespoke to the issues this client is concerned about) which give proof points on your effectiveness and efficiency.
- Testimonials from clients and trusted sources that demonstrate your value or competence in relevant areas, which either reinforce what you know the client regards as your strengths or address perceived weaknesses.

4. Reconnect with the other members of the client's team who weren't in the pitch but who are important influencers. Reach out to procurement or market research and strengthen ties ahead of any possible negotiations. Write to thank any of the clients' advisors or employees who helped you, gave their opinion, showed you around the facilities etc. Saying thank you echoes well.

5. Create new work or send relevant articles, books, papers, synopses of events and other materials that demonstrate care and attention; show you are on the ball and hungry. This is where you activate your social media to help the clients (a) see that you, your team and your organisation are valued thought leaders; (b) be impressed with your intellectual energy; and (c) sense your fit with them.

6. Invite the clients to events that they will find interesting or connect them with stimulating people. (You should have been doing this all the way through the process anyway!)

7. Activate your network to create positive surround sound as the clients are making up their minds. For example, online endorsements and recommendations from existing clients or media commentators.

8. Generate positive PR at the time the clients are considering their options. For example, when we were running a global pitch for a major bank based in Asia, we knew we were vulnerable in their home hub. The

day before the pitch presentation, we read in the *Financial Times* that our rival for the client's business had just made investments in not one, but two companies in that hub. This well-timed coup tipped the balance and we lost. Hats off to the opposition. That's pitch-craft at the highest-stakes level.

You need to do all of this even if you are convinced you knocked the presentation out of the park and have won the business – even if, in marriage terms, you proposed and your intended said 'yes'. This is when your behaviour can get things off to a brilliant start or sabotage future happiness. When Prince Charles and Lady Diana Spencer announced their engagement in 1981, they were interviewed and when the interviewer asked, 'And you're in love?', Diana said, 'Of course'. Prince Charles responded ominously, 'Whatever "love" is.' It was a bombshell and a very peculiar thing for a newly engaged man to say. The world was watching and many could see trouble ahead. Judging by Diana's face when he said it, she could, too. So do not instantly make your client worried or regret they have chosen you.

You have to show you mean what you say. Behave as you did in the room out of the room, too.

Sometimes decision-making is a severa-stage process and can take months. **It can feel like forever when the clients are making up their mind.** You have to go through it with your client step by step, answering questions and concerns, providing additional materials, having further discussions on finances and fees and staffing levels and processes and systems integration and logistics and, and, and ... It can seem as though the rounds of documentation and dialogue are endless. The more work you have done before this stage, the easier it is going to be after the presentation. It is also important to understand from the outset the decision-making process and who will be involved. Be prepared. It might be that you win because you are the last one still standing, the one with the most stamina.

Stay focused on the size of the prize and be disciplined every time you get through to the next stage. Each time, get feedback, adapt and re-commit.

CHAPTER 17
Lose or win – get feedback

Get feedback if you lose. This will improve your next pitch and opens up the possibility of another go or a different assignment from this client. No doesn't mean no for ever. One day, that opportunity will come round again. So take the disappointment soberly, be polite, demonstrate tenacity and determination to fight another day. *And stay in touch.* Don't be a stranger. Go through the whole loop again *until you win*. It might take a few years but this tenacity is what marks out the best pitchers.

Ask things like:

- What worked? Ask for feedback regarding the energy of your team, credibility of expertise, clarity of proposal, performance throughout the process, positives from the presentation.
- Who, on your team, did the clients like and feel is crucial to delivery for them?
- Which areas you covered hit home? Where did you appear light and are, therefore, vulnerable?
- What was going on behind the scenes? We've known pitches where the clients, having been warm all the way through the process, suddenly stiffen for the final presentation and become very poker-faced. Consequently, the presentation meeting feels unusually cold. It was probably not about you. Stuff may have been going on in the background: the CEO may have felt ill and decided to dial in at the last minute rather than be there in person. They may have decided to 'give nothing away' so all the pitching parties could compete on an even playing field.

- What have they learned from the process and how has their thinking evolved?
- Are there some areas that have emerged as more important than other areas? For example, market access in specific geographies or areas of specific expertise they've discovered they need more of. How did your team index on those important areas?
- Are there going to be additional rounds of presentation to address these newer priorities? If so, how long do you have to prepare and what guidance can they give you? If not, ask if you can submit documentation to bolster your case in these areas.

If you win the pitch, ask what tipped the balance in your favour and if the client has any thoughts or suggestions on how you could have been better. It signals a commitment to constant improvement and will give you insight you can act on – for this client and in future pitches for other clients.

CHAPTER 18
When you win

Celebrate with the team. Not merely with the mechanical clinking of glasses or the hollow 'We are delighted to announce ...' Show real appreciation of the victory. Do not let the moment be suffocated by your next deadline. Recognition is not a social courtesy – it creates a shared story for your team and writes a new legend in the organisation. Speak the names of the heroes. Let them hear what they have achieved. Let them remember this feeling of triumph, the happy laughter, the camaraderie. This always makes the team stronger and boosts their appetite to win more and more.

Celebrating your victories properly is important! David has always remembered the CEO at the company he worked for announcing, at the first 'All Hands' meeting of the year, a special award to him and a team of five others. The award was for 'The Best Use of Christmas' when they worked between Christmas and the new year to bring in two new clients, Easy Jeans and Nikon (cameras). It was tongue-in-cheek (they did enjoy time with their families, of course), but it was an acknowledgment that they had gone above and beyond.

Invite the client to celebrate, too. After all, they've just said 'yes' to a relationship together and also had to make several unpleasant calls to your competitors, who lost. When they call you, they know that the moment they hang up, you'll go whooping along the corridor to tell everyone the good news and open the bubbly. Meanwhile, they just get on with their work. So invite them to join you – either virtually or in real life – and celebrate together.

Get off to a racing start

And after a brilliant night out, it's time to agree on the next steps and confirm the details. It is the moment where excitement should give way to structure and consequence.

You sit there, the weight of the win still in the air, but now it's time to talk timelines, deliverables, expectations. Even if you still have a glass of something in hand, you have to make sure the first steps are sure.

The project starts here. Get everyone in the room. It's about business now – the work ahead and how to get it done. Lay out the plan. Keep it simple:

- This is what we're building.
- This is how long it takes.
- This is who does what.

No guessing. No assumptions. Make sure everyone walks out knowing what comes next and their role in making it happen.

Then start moving fast. A win means nothing if the work stalls. Get started. Keep the client in the loop. You need to *over-communicate* at this stage. Not to impress, just to remind them that things are happening, that they made the right choice. Keep pitch-level momentum. Doing this might lead to even more opportunities with these clients. If you want to know how you accelerate the expansion of the business from here, read *The Work Smarter Guide to Sales*. It explores how you grow the relationship and the business now you've won it.

Maintain momentum

It feels good to win, doesn't it? Three wins in a row will tell you you are doing it right. And that will generate its own momentum. Your confidence will be high, and your competition will notice your success and be intimidated when they compete against you. Talent will be attracted your way and potential clients will think they should hear what you have to say. You may even command premium fees to go with your premium pitch performance. Winning itself is persuasive. It's not painless. But it's possible when you do the things in this book every time, all the time, without fail. Do so and luck will follow you.

CHECKLIST

Post-presentation

- [ ] Gather the team immediately – debrief and address any immediate issues.
- [ ] Get instant feedback from your 'mole' – the person you've built the best relationship with at the client or intermediary – both positives and negatives.
- [ ] Respond to the feedback and address any concerns.
- [ ] Be active – connect with all your contacts who can support your cause to surround the client with positive echoes and endorsements while they decide.
- [ ] Create noise on social media and drive positive PR.

If you won the pitch
- [ ] Celebrate with the team.
- [ ] Promptly follow up with the client.
- [ ] Outline the next steps and confirm details.
- [ ] Kick off the project smoothly.
- [ ] Set expectations and clarify roles.
- [ ] Ensure that both your team and the client understand the road map and are excited to begin.
- [ ] Begin work promptly.
- [ ] Update the client regularly to maintain positive momentum.

If you lost the pitch
- [ ] Thank the client for the opportunity and express genuine interest in staying connected. You hope for future opportunities.
- [ ] Ask for feedback to understand why the decision went in a different direction.

- ☐ Maintain contact – consider offering relevant resources, insights or thought leadership that might benefit the client.
- ☐ Reassess your pitch strategy, analyse the client's feedback and consider what might make your future pitching more persuasive.

Acknowledgements

We love pitching. We think it is the most fun you can have at work. And we have learnt so many valuable lessons from the many, many pitches we have each been involved with – both as participants and as advisors. We learnt from the best and have spent countless late nights and weekends working with the brightest people: bosses, peers, specialists, lawyers, accountants, realtors, architects, strategists, brokers, traders, bankers, automotive manufacturers, creatives, consultants, intermediaries, agencies, MBA students, VCs – even angels. Most have imparted wisdom and a few have exhibited folly. We are grateful to them all, for each of them has taught us something which has made our pitching better and more fun. Those who have made it most fun and who have generously helped us create this book by sharing their views, experience, expertise and stories deserve special mention. They are all amazing practitioners of the art of pitching: Seguei Lyovin, Angela Johnson, Ross Sutherland, Tanya Khan, Annette King, Tony Stratton, Keith Jones, Jane Cunningham, Ben Richards, David Mayo, and the much missed and sadly departed John Fowler, Alan Waldie, John Salmon and Chris Cowpe. Thank you. Muchly.

Index

accountants 10
Agarwal, Venkat 59
agendas 37
Amiables 28–32, 34, 36–8, 42–3
Analyticals 26–8, 30–3, 35–8, 41, 65
anecdotes 59
appearance 8
Apprentice, The (TV show) 3, 49
Artificial Intelligence (AI) 53, 63, 72, 112
Attenborough, Richard 3–4
attention spans 104, 107
audiences 17, 63, 102–4, 107

beliefs, shared 57
'big picture' 10, 30
biographies 60–3
Body Shop 57
business-to-business (B2B) 16, 58

Carnegie, Dale 15
challenges 69–71, 78
Charles III, King 122
checklists 13, 41–5, 51, 86–7, 116, 129–30
chemistry 16, 19–20, 60, 99
clarification 66–7
client briefs 64, 65–71
client criteria 53
clients
    aims 21
    decision-making 122
    letting them talk 6
    needs 57–8, 64–5, 77–8, 83
collaboration 3–4, 25, 32, 43, 61, 67, 105
communication 39–43, 103
    explicit 39
    illusion of 68
    implicit 39
    non-verbal 39, 67–8, 103
    and personality styles 41–3
    preferences 23–30

competition 72
connection 58–60, 63
context 59, 67–8, 81–3
control 97–111, 116
conviction 92
Crick, Francis 77
cultural norms 40
culture
    company 40, 68
    high-context 39, 40
    low-context 39
    national 19–20, 38–40, 52, 58, 68
customer behaviours 72

data 41, 75
de Bono, Edward 75
decision-making 27–30, 122
detail management 97–111
Diana, Princess 122
discipline 11–12
Dragon's Den (TV show) 3, 16, 49
Drivers 27–38, 41–2

early, being 8–9, 96
Easy Jeans 57, 126
economics 71–2
Edison, Thomas 117
efficiency 42
Einstein, Albert 64
electric vehicles 70, 72
emotion 10–11, 15, 75
energy levels 114–15
enthusiasm 5–6
environmental issues 72–3
ethics 72–3
evidence 41, 120–1
experience 74–5
experts, curse of 74
Expressives 29–30, 33–8, 43
eye contact 39

INDEX

FAB Method 77–8
facts 75
feedback 120, 124–5
Ford, Henry, Model T 69–70
freshness 74–5
future, painting a picture of 56–7

gestures 39
Google 105

hierarchy 39, 40
Hippocrates 24
hypothesis-testing 77

impression-making 5, 20, 58–63
insiders ('moles') 21–2, 45, 120
inspiration 43
introductions 58–63, 103

Japan 39
jargon 10, 61–2, 113
Jobs, Steve 74

King, Martin Luther 56
King, Stephen 47

language use 115
Lasarte restaurant, Barcelona 105
lawyers 69, 84–5
legislation 73
Lincoln, Abraham, Gettysburg Address 76–7
LinkedIn profiles 33, 34
listening skills 104, 110
logic 41
logic chains 76–7
London Business School, *Launchpad* 59, 77

Martin, Steve 99
mass production 70
McDonald's 63
meetings 7, 16
  and chemistry 16, 19–20
  first 19–22
  as mini-pitches 20
  online 33–4, 44–5, 52
  in person 44–5, 51–2
  preparation for 20–2, 44–5
  and wavelength 31–7, 38, 41–5

Mehrabian, Albert 103
mistake-making 10–11
momentum 127–8
Musk, Elon 72

National Health Service (NHS) 21–2
networking 45
Nikon 126

objectives 37
optimism 75
organisation 11
Orwell, George 112–13
outsiders, involvement 9–10
overviews 75

P&G 50
PECSTEL framework 71–3
people 15–45
  communication preferences 23–30
  first meetings 19–22
  getting on the same wavelength as 31–7
  personality styles 23–38, 41–3, 51, 65
  understanding your 38–40
people to people (P2P) 16
personality styles 23–38, 41–3, 51, 65
perspective 74–5, 76
persuasion 3–4, 91
pessimism 75
photos 60–1
Pitch Playbook 50–1
pitching
  definition 3–4
  and feedback 120, 124–5
  individualising 20–1
  international 52–3
  like a pro 47–87
  local 52
  losing 124–5, 129–30
  online 33–4, 44–5, 51–2
  and people 15–45
  in person 44–5, 51–2
  planning the basics 5–13
  post-pitch 117–30
  postscript 114–16
  and presentations 49, 51–4, 83, 89–116, 120
  and problems 64–73, 78, 86–7
  process of 49–55, 86
  and product 74–8, 87

and profit 79–85, 87
and promise 56–63, 75, 86
winning 115, 125–9
politics 71
post-pitch 117–30
pre-pitch 1–15
presentations 49, 51–4, 82–4, 89–116
and control 97–111, 116
demonstrating what it means to win 115
and energy levels 114–15
and language 115
order of presenting 100–1
Q&A 95, 108–11, 120
room/environment 103, 104–7, 108
and rules/rule-breaking 92–5
showtime 91–6, 103, 105–6
and teams 98–100
and technology 107–8
and timing 37, 102–4
and written pitches 112–13
price 80–4
problems 64–73, 78, 86–7
process 49–55, 86
product 74–8, 87
profit 79–85, 87
promise 56–63, 75, 86
punctuality 8–9
purpose, common 57

Q&A 95, 108–11, 120

reading between the lines 67–8, 110
recency effect 100
rehearsal 54, 114
relationship 43
Request for Proposals (RFP), early submission 96
results 42
Roddick, Anita 57
room/environment 103–8
routines 9

scaling 70
Seinfeld, Jerry 89
Seneca 1
Shakespeare, William 112
Shaw, George Bernard 68
showtime 91–6, 103, 105–6
Six Thinking Hats technique 75–6

small talk 31–2, 37, 39, 52
socio-demographics 72
spell-checking 7–8
standing out 53, 54, 58, 96
story-listening 71
storytelling 37, 71
Sugar, Lord 49
supplementary material 65
SWOT analysis 71

teams
celebrating wins 126
and diversity 22, 38
and introductions 59–60
and personality types 38
post-pitch 119–20
presenting 37, 98–100
résumés 61–3
and togetherness 99–100
uncohesive 97
technology 72, 107–8
TED Talks 104
Tesco 55
Tesla 70, 72
testimonials 121
time issues 37, 102–4
time zones 52–3
transportation 69–70
trust 45, 60

UPS 6, 58, 110

Value Proposition Canvas 77–8
venture capitalists 59, 72, 77
vision 43

Watson, James 77
wavelength 31–7
working from home 52, 105
written communication 67–8, 112–13